AA Essential

Greek
phrase book

AA Publishing

Contents

English edition prepared by First Edition Translations Ltd, Great Britain

Designed and produced by AA Publishing

Distributed in the United Kingdom by AA Publishing, Norfolk House, Priestley Road, Basingstoke, Hampshire RG24 9NY

First published in 1995 as Wat & Hoe Grieks, © Uitgeverij Kosmos bv - Utrecht/Antwerpen

Van Dale Lexicografie bv - Utrecht/Antwerpen

This edition © The Automobile Association 1997
Reprinted Sep 1998

A CIP catalogue record for this book is available from the British Library

ISBN: 0 7495 1473 6

Published by AA Publishing (a trading name of Automobile Association Developments Limited, whose registered office is Norfolk House, Priestley Road, Basingstoke, Hampshire RG24 9NY. Registered number 1878835).

Typeset by Anton Graphics Ltd, Andover, Hampshire.

Printed and bound by G Canale C.Spa, Torino, Italy.

Photocredits for front cover: Olives, AA Photo Library (J. Edmanson); Parliament guard, Athens, Spectrum Colour Library; Erectheion, Athens, Spectrum Colour Library

Introduction

● **Welcome to the AA's new Essential Phrase Books series, covering the most popular European languages and containing everything you'd expect from a comprehensive language series. They're concise, accessible and easy to understand, and you'll find them indispensable on your trip abroad.**

Each guide is divided into 15 themed sections and starts with a pronunciation table which gives you the phonetic spelling to all the words and phrases you'll need to know for your trip, while at the back of the book is an extensive word list and grammar guide which will help you construct basic sentences in your chosen language.

Throughout the book you'll come across coloured boxes with a 🐌 beside them. These are designed to help you if you can't understand what your listener is saying to you. Hand the book over to them and encourage them to point to the appropriate answer to the question you are asking.

Other coloured boxes in the book - this time without the symbol - give alphabetical listings of themed words with their English translations beside them.

For extra clarity, we have put all English words and phrases in black, foreign language terms in red and their phonetic pronunciation in italic.

This phrase book covers all subjects you are likely to come across during the course of your visit, from reserving a room for the night to ordering food and drink at a restaurant and what to do if your car breaks down or you lose your traveller's cheques and money. With over 2,000 commonly used words and essential phrases at your fingertips you can rest assured that you will be able to get by in all situations, so let the Essential Phrase Book become your passport to a secure and enjoyable trip!

Pronunciation table

The sounds of Greek are not particularly easy for an English speaker. In the pronunciation guide given for each word or phrase, the following system is used:

a	somewhere between southern English **a** in **mast** and **u** in **cup**
b	similar to an English **b** but less aggressive
ch	as Scots **ch** in **loch**
d	similar to an English **d** but less agressive
dh	as English **th** in **the**, **this**, **them**
e	as English **e** in **met**
f	as English **f** in **soft**
g	as English **g** in **go**
gh	a difficult sound: try saying a hard English **g** (as in **grab**) as far down your throat as possible.
h	a more breathy form of the English **h** in **hoot**
i	like the **ee** in **feet**, but make the sound more clipped
k	like the English **c** in **cat**
l	as English **l** in **lick**
m	as English **m** in **mat**
n	as English **n** in **not**
ng	just like the **ng** in **English**
o	like the English **o** in **pop**
oo	like the **oo** in English **ooze**
p	a lot less explosive than an English **p**
r	lightly rolled, as in Italian or Scots: keep your tongue much closer to the back of your teeth than in a English **r**
s	as in English **sit**
t	more or less as in English **tap**
th	as English soft **th** in **thistle**
v	as in English **van**
w	as in English **went**
x	as the **x** in **box**
y	not a vowel but a glide, as in **yes**, **you**, **yacht**
z	as in English **zoo** or the **s** at the end of **was**

Note also the following combinations:

n(g)x	somewhere between English **things** and **thinks**
n(g)ch	as in the middle of **melancholy**

Stress and accents

In the pronunciation guide the stresses are marked with an accent, e.g. **o patéras** (father). The vowel **ou** is transcribed as **oo** when not stressed and **óo** when stressed. Any two other vowels together in the transcription must be pronounced separately, e.g. **aerodhrómyo** must be pronounced **a-e-rodhrómyo**, as must **oó**, which indicates two independent adjacent **o** sounds.

Useful lists

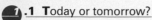

1.1 **T**oday or tomorrow?

What day is it today? _____	Τί μέρα είναι σήμερα;
	Ti méra íne símera?
Today's Monday_____	Σήμερα είναι Δευτέρα
	Símera íne dheftéra
– Tuesday_____	Σήμερα είναι Τρίτη
	Símera íne tríti
– Wednesday _____	Σήμερα είναι Τετάρτη
	Símera íne tetárti
– Thursday_____	Σήμερα είναι Πέμπτη
	Símera íne pémpti
– Friday_____	Σήμερα είναι Παρασκευή
	Símera íne paraskeví
– Saturday _____	Σήμερα είναι Σάββατο
	Símera íne sávato
– Sunday _____	Σήμερα είναι Κυριακή
	Símera íne kiriakí
in January _____	τον Ιανουάριο
	ton yanooário
since February _____	από το Φεβρουάριο
	apó to fevrooário
in spring_____	την άνοιξη
	tin ánixi
in summer_____	το καλοκαίρι
	to kalokyéri
in autumn _____	το φθινόπωρο
	to fthinóporo
in winter_____	το χειμώνα
	to himóna
1997_____	χίλια εννιακόσια εννενήντα εφτά
	hília enyakósia enenínda eftá
the twentieth century_____	τον εικοστό αιώνα
	ton ikostó eóna
What's the date today? ____	Τί ημερομηνία έχουμε σήμερα/Πόσες του
	μηνός έχουμε σήμερα;
	ti imerominía éhome símera/póses too
	minós éhome símera?
Today's the 24th_____	Σήμερα είναι 24 του μηνός
	símera íne ikositéseres too minós
Monday 8 November _____	Δευτέρα, 8 Νοεμβρίου 1998
1998	*dheftéra ochtó noemvríoo hília enyakósia*
	enenínda ochtó
in the morning _____	το πρωί
	to proí
in the afternoon_____	το μεσημέρι
	to mesiméri
in the evening _____	το βράδυ
	to vrádhi
at night_____	τη νύχτα
	ti níchta
this morning _____	σήμερα το πρωί
	símera to proí

this afternoon	σήμερα το μεσημέρι
	símera to mesiméri
this evening	σήμερα το απόγευμα
	símera to apógevma
tonight	απόψε
	apópse
last night	την περασμένη νύχτα
	timberasméni níchta
this week	αυτή την εβδομάδα
	avtí tin evdhomádha
next month	τον επόμενο μήνα
	ton epómeno mína
last year	πέρυσι
	périsi
next...	τον επόμενο.../την επόμενη.../το επόμενο...
	ton epómeno.../tin epómeni.../to epómeno...
in...days/weeks/ months/years	σε...μέρες/εβδομάδες/μήνες/χρόνια
	se...méres/evdhomádhes/hrónia
...weeks ago	πριν από... εβδομάδες
	prin apó...evdhomádhes
day off	αργία
	aryía

.2 Bank holidays

● **The most important** public holidays in Greece are the following:

January 1	(New Year's Day) Η Πρωτοχρονιά
January 6	(Epiphany) Τα Επιφάνια
March 25	(The anniversary of the start of the War of Independence against the Turks in 1826) Εικοστή Πέμπτη Μαρτίου
April/May	(Easter: Greek Easter is celebrated according to the Orthodox Church calendar, and occurs on different dates from British Easter) Πάσχα
May 1	(May Day, Labour Day) Πρωτομαγιά
May/June	(Ascension; Whit Sunday) Της Αναλήψεως
August 15	(Assumption) Η Κοίμησις της Θεοτόκου
October 28	("No! Day": the day on which the Greeks refused the Italian ultimatum in 1940) Εικοστή Ογδόη Οκτωβρίου
December 25	(Christmas) Χριστούγεννα

Most shops, banks and government institutions are closed on these days. Good Friday and Boxing Day are not bank holidays.

.3 What time is it?

What time is it?	Τί ώρα είναι;
	ti óra íne?
It's nine o'clock	Είναι εννιά
	íne enyá
– five past ten	Είναι δέκα και πέντε
	íne dhéka ke pénde
– a quarter past eleven	Είναι έντεκα και τέταρτο
	íne éndeka ke tétarto
– twenty past twelve	Είναι δώδεκα και είκοσι
	íne dhódheka ke íkosi

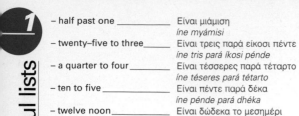

– half past one	Είναι μιάμιση	*íne myámisi*
– twenty–five to three	Είναι τρεις παρά είκοσι πέντε	*íne tris pará íkosi pénde*
– a quarter to four	Είναι τέσσερες παρά τέταρτο	*íne téseres pará tétarto*
– ten to five	Είναι πέντε παρά δέκα	*íne pénde pará dhéka*
– twelve noon	Είναι δώδεκα το μεσημέρι	*íne dhódheka to mesiméri*
– midnight	Είναι μεσάνυχτα	*íne mesánichta*
half an hour	μισή ώρα	*misí óra*
What time?	Τί ώρα;	*ti óra?*
What time can I come round?	Τί ώρα μπορώ να περάσω;	*ti óra boró na peráso?*
At...	Στις...	*stis...*
After...	Μετά τις...	*metá tis...*
Before...	Πριν από τις...	*prin apó tis...*
Between...and...	Μεταξύ...και...	*metaxí... ke...*
From...to...	Από τις...μέχρι τις...	*apó tis... méhri tis...*
In...minutes	Σε...λεπτά	*se...leptá*
– ...hours	Σε...ώρες	*se...óres*
– a quarter of an hour	Σ΄ ένα τέταρτο	*s' éna tétarto*
– three quarters of an hour	Σε τρία τέταρτα	*se tría tétarta*
early	πολύ νωρίς	*polí norís*
on time	στην ώρα	*stin óra*
summertime	θερινή ώρα	*theriní óra*
wintertime	χειμερινή ώρα	*himeriní óra*

1.4 One, two, three...

zero	μηδέν	*midhén*
1	ένα	*éna*
2	δύο	*dhío*
3	τρία	*tría*
4	τέσσερα	*téssera*
5	πέντε	*pénde*
6	έξι	*éxi*
7	εφτά	*eftá*
8	οχτώ	*ochtó*
9	εννιά	*enyá*

10	δέκα	*dhéka*
11	ένδεκα	*éndheka*
12	δώδεκα	*dhódheka*
13	δεκατρία	*dhekatría*
14	δεκατέσσερα	*dhekatésera*
15	δεκαπέντε	*dhekapénde*
16	δεκαέξι	*dhekaéxi*
17	δεκαεφτά	*dhekaeftá*
18	δεκαοχτό	*dhekaochtó*
19	δεκαεννιά	*dekhaenyá*
20	είκοσι	*íkosi*
21	είκοσι ένα	*kosi éna*
22	είκοσι δύο	*íkosi dhío*
30	τριάντα	*triánda*
31	τριάντα ένα	*triánda éna*
32	τριάντα δύο	*triánda dhío*
40	σαράντα	*saránda*
50	πενήντα	*penínda*
60	εξήντα	*exínda*
70	εβδομήντα	*evdhomínda*
80	ογδοντα	*oghdhónda*
90	εννενήντα	*enenínda*
100	εκατό	*ekató*
101	εκατόν ένα	*ekatón éna*
110	εκατό δέκα	*ekató dhéka*
120	εκατόν είκοσι	*ekatón íkosi*
200	διακόσια	*dhiakósia*
300	τριακόσια	*triakósia*
400	τετρακόσια	*tetrakósia*
500	πεντακόσια	*pendakósia*
600	εξακόσια	*exakósia*
700	εφτακόσια	*eftakósia*
800	οχτακόσια	*ochtakósia*
900	εννιακόσια	*enyakósia*
1000	χίλια	*hílya*
1100	χίλια εκατό	*hílya ekató*
2000	δύο χιλιάδες	*dhío hilyádhes*
10,000	δέκα χιλιάδες	*dhéka hilyádhes*
100,000	εκατό χιλιάδες	*ekató hilyádhes*
1,000,000	ένα εκατομμύριο	*éna ekatomírio*
1st	πρώτος	*prótos*
2nd	δεύτερος	*dhéfteros*
3rd	τρίτος	*trítos*
4th	τέταρτος	*tétartos*
5th	πέμπτος	*pémptos*
6th	έκτος	*éktos*
7th	έβδομος	*évdhomos*
8th	όγδοος	*óghdhoos*
9th	ένατος	*énatos*
10th	δέκατος	*dhékatos*
11th	ενδέκατος	*endhékatos*
12th	δωδέκατος	*dhodhékatos*

13th	δέκατος τρίτος	*dhékatos trítos*
14th	δέκατος τέταρτος	*dhékatos tétartos*
15th	δέκατος πέμπτος	*dhékatos pémptos*
16th	δέκατος έκτος	*dhékatos éktos*
17th	δέκατος έβδομος	*dhékatos évdhomos*
18th	δέκατος όγδοος	*dhékatos óghdhoos*
19th	δέκατος ένατος	*dhékatos énatos*
20th	εικοστός	*ikostós*
21st	εικοστός πρώτος	*kostós prótos*
22nd	εικοστός δεύτερος	*ikostós dhéfteros*
30th	τριανταкоστός	*triandakostós*
100th	εκατοστός	*ekatostós*
1000th	χιλιοστός	*hilyostós*

once	μία φορά
	mía forá
twice	δύο φορές
	dhío forés
double	το διπλό
	to dhipló
triple	το τριπλάσιο
	to triplásio
half	το μισό
	to misó
a quarter	ένα τέταρτο
	éna tétarto
a third	ένα τρίτο
	éna tríto
a few, some	μερικά
	meriká

2+4=6	δύο και τέσσερα ίσον έξι
	dhío ke tésera íson éxi
4-2=2	τέσσερα μείον δύο ίσον δύο
	tésera míon dhío íson dhío
2x4=8	δύο επί τέσσερα ίσον οχτώ
	dhío epí tésera íson ochtó
4÷2=2	τέσσερα διά δύο ίσον δύο
	tésera dhía dhío íson dhío
odd/even	μονός/ζυγός
	mónos/zighós
total	συνολικά
	sinoliká
6x9	έξι επί εννιά
	éxi epí enyá

1.5 The weather

Is the weather going to be good/bad?	Θα έχουμε καλό/κακό καιρό;
	tha éhoome kaló/kakó kyeró?
Is it going to get colder/hotter?	Θα κάνει περισσότερο κρύο/περισσότερη ζέστη;
	tha káni perisótero krío/perisóteri zésti?
What temperature is it going to be?	Τί θερμοκρασία θα κάνει σήμερα;
	ti thermokrasía tha káni símera?
Is it going to rain?	Θα βρέξει;
	tha vréxi?

Is there going to be a _____ storm?	Θα έχουμε θύελλα; *tha éhoome thíela?*
Is it going to snow? _____	Θα χιονίσει; *tha hyonísi?*
Is it going to freeze? _____	Θα κάνει παγωνιά; *tha káni pagonyá?*
Is the thaw setting in? _____	Θα λιώσουν τα χιόνια; *tha lyósoon ta hyónya?*
Is it going to be foggy? ____	Θα πέσει ομίχλη; *tha pési omíchli?*
Is there going to be a _____ thunderstorm?	Θα έχουμε καταιγίδα; *tha éhoome kateyídha?*
The weather's changing ___	Αλλάζει ο καιρός *alázi o kyerós*
It's cooling down _____	Δροσίζει *dhrosízi*
What's the weather_____ going to be like today/ tomorrow?	Τί καιρό θα έχουμε σήμερα/αύριο; *ti kyéro tha éhoome símera/ávrio?*

.6 Here, there...

See also 5.1 Asking for directions

here/there _____	εδώ/εκεί *edhó/ekí*
somewhere/nowhere _____	κάπου/πουθενά *kápou/poothená*
everywhere _____	παντού *pandóo*
far away/nearby_____	μακριά/κοντά *makriá/kondá*
to the right/left _____	προς τα δεξιά/αριστερά *pros ta dhexyá/aristerá*
on the right/left of _____	δεξιά/αριστερά από *dhexyá/aristerá apó*
straight ahead _____	ίσια *ísya*
via _____	μέσω *méso*
in _____	σε *se*
on_____	πάνω σε *páno se*
under _____	κάτω από *káto apó*
against _____	εναντίον *enandíon*
opposite_____	απέναντι *apénandi*
next to/near_____	δίπλα σε/κοντά σε *dhípla se/kondá se*
in front of_____	μπροστά *brostá*
in the centre _____	στη μέση *sti mési*

άνεμος **wind**	ελαφρές νεφώσεις **light cloud**	ομίχλη **mist/fog**
ανέφελος **cloudless**	ζεστός **hot**	παγετός **frost**
αποπνικτικός **muggy/** **oppressive**	ηλιόλουστο **sunny**	ριπέςαέρα **gusts of wind**
αφόρητη ζέστη **unbearable heat**	θύελλα **storm**	συννεφιά **cloudy**

...βαθμοί κάτω/πάνω
  από το μηδέν
...degrees
  below/above
  zero
	καλός
	fine
		τσουχτερός
		bitingly
		  cold

	καύσωνας **heatwave**	τυφώνας **cyclone**
	μαλακός/ήπιος **mild**	φυσάει **it is windy**

βαριές νεφώσεις
heavy cloud
	μέτριος/δυνατός
	  άνεμος
	medium/strong
	  winds
		χαλάζι
		hail

βροχερός **damp**		χιόνι **snow**
βροχή **rain**	μισοσυννεφιασμένος **partly cloudy**	ψυχρός **very cold**
δροσερός **cool**	μπόρα **squall of rain**	

forward _____ εμπρός/προς τα εμπρός
embrós/pros ta embrós

down _____ (προς τα) κάτω
(pros ta) káto

up _____ (προς τα) πάνω
(pros ta) páno

inside _____ (προς τα) μέσα
(pros ta) mésa

outside _____ (προς τα) έξω
(pros ta) éxo

behind _____ (προς τα) πίσω
(pros ta) píso

at the front _____ μπροστά
brostá

at the back _____ πίσω - πίσω
píso-píso

in the north _____ στο βορρά
sto vorá

to the south _____ προς το νότο
pros to nóto

from the west _____ από τη δύση
apó ti dhísi

from the east _____ της ανατολής
tis anatolís

north/south/west/east of ___ βόρεια/νότια/δυτικά/
ανατολικά από
vórya/nótya/dhitiká/
anatolitiká apó

14

See also 5.4 Traffic signs.

ΑΝΔΡΩΝ
gents

ΑΝΕΛΚΥΣΤΗΡΑΣ
lift

ΑΝΟΙΧΤΟ/ΚΛΕΙΣΤΟ
open/shut

ΑΠΑΓΟΡΕΥΕΤΑΙ Η
ΕΙΣΟΔΟΣ
no entry

ΑΠΑΓΟΡΕΥΕΤΑΙ Η
ΦΩΤΟΓΡΑΦΗΣΗ
no photography

ΑΠΑΓΟΡΕΥΕΤΑΙ ΝΑ
ΠΑΤΑΤΕ ΣΤΟ
ΓΡΑΣΙΔΙ
do not walk on the
grass

ΑΠΑΓΟΡΕΥΕΤΑΙ ΤΟ
ΚΑΠΝΙΣΜΑ
no smoking

ΑΠΑΓΟΡΕΥΟΝΤΑΙ ΤΑ
ΚΑΤΟΙΚΙΔΙΑ ΖΩΑ
no pets

ΑΠΟΧΩΡΗΤΗΡΙΑ/
ΤΟΥΑΛΕΤΤΕΣ
lavatories/toilets

ΓΥΝΑΙΚΩΝ
ladies

ΕΔΩ
ΠΛΗΡΟΦΟΡΙΕΣ
information desk

ΕΙΣΟΔΟΣ
entrance

ΕΚΠΤΩΣΕΙΣ
reduction/sale

ΕΚΤΟΣ ΛΕΙΤΟΥΡΓΙΑΣ
out of order

ΕΛΕΥΘΕΡΗ
ΕΙΣΟΔΟΣ
free entry

ΕΝΟΙΚΙΑΖΕΤΑΙ
to let

ΕΞΟΔΟΣ
exit

ΕΞΟΔΟΣ ΚΙΝΔΥΝΟΥ
emergency exit

ΙΔΙΟΚΤΗΣΙΑ
private/private
property

ΚΙΝΔΥΝΟΣ
danger

ΚΙΝΔΥΝΟΣ ΘΑΝΑΤΟΥ
danger!

ΚΙΝΔΥΝΟΣ
ΠΥΡΚΑΓΙΑΣ
fire hasard

ΚΛΕΙΣΜΕΝΟ/
ΡΕΖΕΡΒΕ
booked/reserved

ΚΥΛΙΟΜΕΝΗ
ΣΚΑΛΑ
escalator

ΜΗ ΠΟΣΙΜΟ ΝΕΡΟ
no drinking water

ΜΗΝ ΑΓΓΙΖΕΤΕ
do not touch

ΜΗΝ ΕΝΟΧΛΕΙΤΕ
do not disturb

ΟΡΟΦΟΣ
floor

ΠΛΗΡΕΣ
full

ΠΛΗΡΟΦΟΡΙΕΣ
information

ΠΡΟΣΟΧΗ ΒΑΦΗ
wet paint

ΠΡΟΣΟΧΗ ΣΚΥΛΟΣ
beware of the dog

ΠΡΟΣΟΧΗ ΤΟ
ΣΚΑΛΙ
mind the step

ΠΡΩΤΕΣ ΒΟΗΘΕΙΕΣ
accident and
emergency service

ΠΩΛΕΙΤΑΙ
for sale

ΡΕΣΕΨΙΟΝ
reception

ΣΗΜΑ ΚΙΝΔΥΝΟΥ
emergency
cord/alarm button

ΣΚΑΛΑ
stairs

ΣΚΑΛΑ ΠΥΡΚΑΓΙΑΣ
fire escape

ΣΥΡΑΤΕ/ΩΘΗΣΑΤΕ
pull/push

ΤΑΜΕΙΟ
cash desk/booking
office

ΥΓΡΟ
damp

ΥΨΗΛΗ ΤΑΣΙΣ
high tension
cables/high
voltage

ΞΕΠΟΥΛΗΜΑ
clearance sale

ΩΡΕΣ
ΛΕΙΤΟΥΡΓΙΑΣ
opening hours

1.8 Telephone alphabet

α	_____	*álfa*	Αλέξανδρος Aléxandhros
β	_____	*víta*	Βασίλιος Vasílyos
γ	_____	*gháma*	Γεώργιος Yeóryos
δ	_____	*dhélta*	Δημήτριος Dhimítrios
ε	_____	*épsilon*	Ελένη Eléni
ζ	_____	*zíta*	Ζωή Zoí

15

η_____	*íta*	Ηρακλής	*Iraklís*
θ_____	*thíta*	Θεόδωρος	*Theódhoros*
ι_____	*yóta*	Ιωάννης	*Yoánis*
κ_____	*kápa*	Κωνσταντίνος	*Konstandínos*
λ_____	*lámdha*	Λεωνίδας	*Leonídhas*
μ_____	*mi*	Μενέλαος	*Menélaos*
ν_____	*ni*	Νικόλαος	*Nikólaos*
ξ_____	*xi*	Ξενοφών	*Xenofón*
ο_____	*ómikron*	Οδυσσέας	*Odhiséas*
π_____	*pi*	Περικλής	*Periklís*
ρ_____	*ro*	Ρόδος	*Ródhos*
σ_____	*síghma*	Σωτήριος	*Sotiríos*
τ_____	*taf*	Τιμολέων	*Timoléon*
υ_____	*ípsilon*	Υψηλάντης	*Ipsilándis*
φ_____	*fi*	Φώτιος	*Fótyos*
χ_____	*hi*	Χρήστος	*Chrístos*
ψ_____	*psi*	Ψάλτης	*Psáltis*
ω_____	*omégha*	Ωμέγα	*Omégha*

1 .9 Personal details

surname_____ επώνυμο
epónimo
christian name(s)_____ (μικρό) όνομα
(mikró) ónoma
initials_____ τα αρχικά
ta arhiká
address (street/number) ___ η διεύθυνση (οδός / αριθμός)
dhiéfthinsi (odhós/arithmós)
post code/town _____ ταχυδρομικός κώδικας / αριθμός κατοικίας
tahidhromikós kódikas/tópos katikías
sex (male/female) _____ φύλο (άρρεν / θήλυ)
fílo (áren/thíli)
nationality_____ υπηκοότητα
ipikoótita
date of birth _____ ημερομηνία γεννήσεως
imerominía yeníseos
place of birth _____ τόπος γεννήσεως
tópos yeníseos

occupation_____	επάγγελμα
	epàngelma
married/single/divorced____	έγγαμος / άγαμος / διεζευγμένος
	éngamos/àgamos/dhiezevgménos
widowed _____	εν χηρεία
	en hiría
(number of) children _____	τέκνα (αριθμός τέκνων)
	tékna (arithmós téknon)
passport/identity _____	αριθμός ταυτότητας διαβατηρίου / άδειας
card/driving licence	οδηγήσεως
number	*arithmós taftótitas dhiavatíryoo/ádhias*
	odhiyíseos
place and date of issue ____	τόπος και ημερομηνία έκδοσης
	tópos ke imerominía ékdhosis

Courtesies

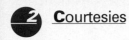

Courtesies

● **It is usual in Greece** for friends and relatives of both sexes to kiss each other on both cheeks when meeting and parting company. People who know each other less well shake hands instead.

.1 Greetings

Hello, Mr Smith _____	Γειά σας κύριε Σμιθ
	ya sas kírie Smith
Hello, Mrs Jones _____	Γειά σας κυρία Ντζωνς
	Ya sas kiría Jones
Hello, Peter _____	Γειά σου Πέτρο
	ya soo Pétro
Hi, Helen _____	Γειά σου Ελένη
	ya soo Eléni
Good morning, madam____	Καλημέρα κυρία
	kaliméra kiría
Good afternoon, sir _____	Καλησπέρα κύριε
	kalispéra kírie
Good evening_____	Καλησπέρα
	kalispéra
How are you? _____	Τί κάνετε;
	ti kánete
Finc, thank you, and you?__	Καλά, κι εσείς;
	kalá kyesís?
Very well _____	Πολύ καλά
	polí kalá
Not very well _____	Οχι και τόσο καλά
	óhi ke tóso kalá
Not too bad_____	Ετσι κι έτσι...
	étsi kyétsi
I'd better be going_____	Φεύγω τώρα
	févgo tóra
I have to be going _____	Πρέπει να φύγω τώρα
	prépi na fígo tóra
Someone's waiting _____ for me Bye!	Με περιμένουν. Γεια σας !
	Me periménoon. Ya sas!
Goodbye _____	Αντίο
	adío
See you later _____	Θα σε δω αργότερα
	tha se dho argótera
See you in a little while___	Θα σε δω σε λίγο
	tha se dho se lígho
Sleep well _____	Καλό ύπνο
	kaló ípno
Good night _____	Καληνύχτα
	kaliníchta
All the best _____	Στο καλό να πας/όλα καλά
	sto kaló na pas/ óla kalá
Have fun_____	Καλή διασκέδαση
	kalí dhiaskédhasi
Good luck _____	Καλή επιτυχία
	kalí epitihía

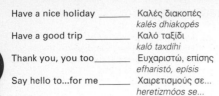

Have a nice holiday	Καλές διακοπές
	kalés dhiakopés
Have a good trip	Καλό ταξίδι
	kaló taxdíhi
Thank you, you too	Ευχαριστώ, επίσης
	efharistó, epísis
Say hello to...for me	Χαιρετισμούς σε...
	heretizmóos se...

.2 How to ask a question

Who?	Ποιός
	pyós?
Who's that?	Ποιός είναι;
	pyós íne?
What?	Τί;
	ti?
What's there to see here?	Τί αξιοθέατα έχει εδώ;
	ti axiothéata éhi edhó?
What kind of hotel is that?	Τί είδος ξενοδοχείο είναι αυτό;
	ti ídhos xenodhohío íne aftó?
What time is it?	Τί ώρα είναι;
	ti óra íne?
Where?	Πού;
	poo?
Where's the toilet?	Πού είναι η τουαλέτα;
	poo íne i twaléta?
Where are you going?	Πού πηγαίνετε;
	poo piyénete?
Where are you from?	Από πού έρχεσθε;
	apó poo érhesthe?
How?	Πώς;
	pos?
How far is that?	Πόσο μακριά είναι;
	póso makriá íne?
How long does that take?	Πόση ώρα διαρκεί/κρατάει;
	pósi óra dhiarkí/kratái?
How long is the trip?	Πόσο κρατάει το ταξίδι;
	póso kratái to taxídhi?
How much?	Πόσος;
	pósos
How much is this?	Πόσο κάνει;
	póso káni?
Which?	Ποιό; Ποιά;
	pyo? pya?
Which glass is mine?	Ποιό ποτήρι είναι δικό μου;
	pyo potíri íne dhikó moo?
When?	Πότε;
	póte?
When are you leaving?	Πότε φεύγετε;
	póte févyete?
Why?	Γιατί;
	yatí?
Could you...me?	Μπορείτε να με... ;
	boríte na me...?
Could you help me, please?	Μπορείτε να με βοηθήσετε, παρακαλώ;
	boríte na me voithísete, parakaló?

Could you point that _____ out to me?	Μπορείτε να μου το δείξετε; *boríte na moo to dhíxete?*
Could you come _____ with me, please?	Μπορείτε να 'ρθείτε μαζί μου, παρακαλώ; *boríte narthíte mazí moo, parakaló?*
Could you..._____	Θέλετε...;/Μπορείτε... ; *thélete...?/Boríte...?*
Could you reserve some _____ tickets for me, please?	Μπορείτε να μου κλείσετε εισιτήρια, παρακαλώ; *boríte na moo klísete isitíria parakaló?*
Do you know...? _____	Ξέρετε...; *xérete...?*
Do you know another _____ hotel, please?	Μήπως ξέρετε κανένα άλλο ξενοδοχείο; *mípos xérete kanéna álo xenodhohío*
Do you have...? _____	Μήπως έχετε...; *mípos éhete...?*
Do you have a...?_____	Μπορείτε να μου δώσετε ένα...; *boríte na moo dhósete éna...?*
Do you have a _____ vegetarian dish, please?	Μήπως έχετε φαγητό χωρίς κρέας; *mípos éhete faitó chorís kréas?*
I'd like... _____	Θα ήθελα... *tha íthela...*
I'd like a kilo of apples, _____ please.	Θα ήθελα ένα κιλό μήλα *tha íthela éna kiló míla*
Can I...?_____	Μπορώ... ; *boró...?*
Can I take this?_____	Μπορώ να το πάρω μαζί μου; *boró na to páro mazí moo?*
Can I smoke here?_____	Μπορώ να καπνίσω εδώ; *boró na kapníso edhó?*
Could I ask you _____ something?	Μπορώ να ρωτήσω κάτι; *boró na rotíso káti?*

2.3 How to reply

Yes, of course _____	Ναι, βέβαια/Βεβαίως *ne, vévea/vevéos*
No, I'm sorry_____	Όχι, λυπάμαι *óhi, lipáme*
Yes, what can I do _____ for you?	Ορίστε *oríste*
Just a moment, please _____	Μια στιγμή/Ένα λεπτό, παρακαλώ *mya stighmí/éna leptó parakaló*
No, I don't have _____ time now	Όχι, δε με βολεύει τώρα *óhi dhen me volévi tóra*
No, that's impossible _____	Όχι, δε γίνεται *óhi, dhe yínete*
I think so _____	Νομίζω *nomízo*
I agree_____	Κι εγώ το νομίζω *kyeghó to nomízo*
I hope so too_____	Κι εγώ το ελπίζω *kyeghó to elpízo*
No, not at all_____	Όχι, καθόλου *óhi kathóloo*
No, no one _____	Όχι, κανένας *óhi kanénas*

No, nothing	Οχι, τίποτα
	óhi típota
That's (not) right	Ετσι είναι / (Δεν) είναι έτσι
	étsi íne/(dhen) íne étsi
I (don't) agree	(Δε) συμφωνώ μαζί σας
	(dhe) simfonó mazí sas
All right	Καλά
	kalá
Okay	Εντάξει
	endáxi
Perhaps	Ισως/Μπορεί
	ísos/borí
I don't know	Δεν ξέρω
	dhen xéro

2.4 Thank you

Thank you	Ευχαριστώ
	efcharistó
You're welcome	Παρακαλώ
	parakaló
Thank you very much	Ευχαριστώ πολύ
	efcharistó polí
Very kind of you	Πολύ ευγενικό εκ μέρους σας
	polí evyenikó ek méroos sas
I enjoyed it very much	Χάρηκα πολύ
	chárika polí
Thank you for your trouble	Ευχαριστώ για τον κόπο
	efcharistó ya tongópo
You shouldn't have	Δεν ήταν ανάγκη
	dhen ítan anángi
That's all right	Δεν πειράζει
	dhembirázi

2.5 Sorry

Sorry!	Συγγνώμη
	sighnómi
Excuse me	Με συγχωρείτε
	me sinchoríte
I'm sorry, I didn't know...	Συγγνώμη, δεν ήξερα ότι...
	sighnómi dhen íxera óti...
I do apologise	Με συγχωρείτε
	me sinchoríte
I'm sorry	Λυπάμαι
	lipáme
I didn't do it on purpose, it was an accident	Δεν τό 'κανα επίτηδες, έγινε κατά λάθος
	dhen tókana epítidhes, éyine katá láthos
Never mind	Εντάξει έτσι
	endáxi étsi
It could've happened to anyone	Αυτό μπορεί να συμβεί στον καθένα
	aftó borí na simví stongathéna

.6 What do you think?

Which do you prefer? _____ Τί προτιμάτε;
ti protimáte?

Do you like it? _____ Σου αρέσει;
soo arési?

Don't you like dancing? ___ Δε σ' αρέσει να χορεύεις;
dhe sarési na chorévis?

I don't mind _____ Το ίδιο μου κάνει
to ídhyo moo káni

Well done! _____ Μπράβο!
brávo

Not bad! _____ Οχι άσχημο!
óhi áschimo!

Great! _____ Υπέροχο!
ipérocho!

Wonderful! _____ θαυμάσιο!
thavmásio!

It's really nice here! _____ Τι ωραία που είναι εδώ!
ti oréa poo íne edhó!

How nice! _____ Τι ωραίο!
ti oréo!

How nice for you! _____ Χαίρομαι για σας!
hérome ya sas!

I'm (not) very _____ (Δεν) είμαι πολύ ευχαριστημένος/
happy with... ευχαριστημένη με...
*(dhen) íme polí efcharistiménos/
efcharistiméni me...*

I'm glad that... _____ Χαίρομαι που...
hérome poo ...

I'm having a great time ____ Περνάω μια χαρά
pernáo mya chará

I'm looking forward to it ___ Περιμένω ανυπόμονα
periméno anipómona

I hope it'll work out _____ Ελπίζω να πετύχει
elpízo na petíhi

What a mess! _____ Τί χάλια!
ti hálya!

That's terrible! _____ Τί απαίσιο!
ti apésyo!

What a pity! _____ Τί κρίμα!
ti kríma!

That's filthy! _____ Τί αηδία!
ti aidhía!

What a load of rubbish! ___ Τί ανοησίες/σαχλαμάρες!
ti anoisíes/sachlamáres!

I don't like... _____ Δε μου αρέσει...
dhe moo arési...

I'm bored to death _____ Πλήττω φοβερά...
plíto foverá

I've had enough_____ Βαρέθηκα πια
varéthika pya

I can't take any more _____ Δεν το ανέχομαι άλλο
of this *dhen to anéchome álo*

I was expecting _____ Περίμενα κάτι τελείως διαφορετικό
something completely *perímena káti telíos dhyaforetikó*
different

Conversation

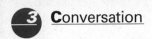

3 Conversation

3.1 I beg your pardon?

I don't speak any/ _____	Δε μιλάω/μιλάω λίγα...
I speak a little...	*dhe miláo/miláo lígha...*
I'm English _____	Είμαι Άγγλος/Αγγλίδα
	íme ánglos/anglídha
I'm Scottish _____	Είμαι Σκωτσέζος/Σκωτσέζα
	íme scotsézos/scotséza
I'm Irish _____	Είμαι Ιρλανδός/Ιρλανδέζα
	íme irlandhós/irlandhéza
I'm Welsh _____	Είμαι Ουαλλός/Ουαλλή
	íme walós/walí
Do you speak _____	Μιλάτε αγγλικά/γαλλικά/γερμανικά;
English/French/German?	*miláte angliká/ghaliká/yermaniká?*
Is there anyone who _____	Ξέρει κανείς εδώ... ;
speaks...?	*xéri kanís edhó...?*
I beg your pardon? _____	Ορίστε;/Τί είπατε;
	oríste?/ti ípate?
I (don't) understand _____	(Δεν) καταλαβαίνω
	(dhen) katalavéno
Do you understand me? ___	Με καταλαβαίνετε;
	me katalavénete?
Could you repeat that, _____	Μπορείτε να το επαναλάβετε, παρακαλώ;
please?	*boríte na to epanalávete, parakaló;*
Could you speak more _____	Μπορείτε να μιλάτε πιο αργά, παρακαλώ;
slowly, please?	*boríte na miláte pyo arghá, parakaló?*
What does that (word) _____	Τί θα πει αυτό/αυτή η λέξη;
mean?	*ti tha pi aftó/aftí i léxi?*
Is that similar to/the _____	Είναι (περίπου) το ίδιο με... ;
same as...?	*íne (perípoo) to ídhyo me...?*
Could you write that _____	Μου το γράφετε, παρακαλώ;
down for me, please?	*moo to ghráfete, parakaló?*
Could you spell that _____	Μου το συλλαβίζετε, παρακαλώ;
for me, please?	*moo to silavízete, parakaló?*

(See 1.8 Telephone alphabet)

Could you point that _____	Μπορείτε να το δείξετε σ' αυτό τον οδηγό;
out in this phrase book,	*boríte na to díxete saftó tonodhighó?*
please?	
One moment, please, _____	Ένα λεπτό, πρέπει να το ψάξω πρώτα
I have to look it up	*éna leptó, prépi na to psáxo próta*
I can't find the word/the ___	Δεν μπορώ να βρω τη λέξη/τη φράση
sentence	*dhemboró na vro ti léxi/ti frási*
How do you say _____	Πώς λέγεται αυτό στα... ;
that in...?	*pos léyete aftó sta...?*
How do you pronounce _____	Πώς προφέρεται αυτό;
that?	*pos proférete aftó?*

3 .2 Introductions

May I introduce myself? ___	Επιτρέψτε μου να συστηθώ
	epitrépste moo na sistithó
My name's... _____	Λέγομαι.../Με λένε...
	léghome.../me léne...
I'm... _____	Είμαι...ο/η
	íme...o/i
What's your name? _____	Πώς λέγεσθε; / Πώς σας λένε;
	pos léyesthe?/ pos sas léne?
May I introduce...? _____	Επιτρέψτε μου να σας συστήσω
	epitrépste moo na sas sistíso
This is my wife/ _____	Αυτή είναι η γυναίκα μου/η κόρη μου/η
daughter/mother/	μητέρα μου/η φίλη μου
girlfriend	*aftí íne i yinéka moo/i kóri moo/i mitéra moo/i*
	fíli moo
– my husband/son/ _____	Αυτός είναι ο άντρας μου/ο γιός μου/ο
father/boyfriend	πατέρας μου/ο φίλος μου
	aftós íne o ándras moo/ o yos moo/o patéras
	moo/o fílos moo
How do you do _____	Γειά σας, χαίρομαι για τη γνωριμία σας
	ya sas, hérome ya ti ghnorimía sas
Pleased to meet you _____	Χαίρω πολύ
	héro polí
Where are you from? _____	Από πού είστε;
	apó poo íste?
I'm from _____	Είμαι απ' την Αγγλία/τη Σκωτία/την
England/Scotland/	Ιρλανδία/την Ουαλία
Ireland/Wales	*íme apó tin anglía/ti scotía/*
	tin irlandhía/tin walía
What city do you live in? ___	Σε ποιά πόλη μένετε;
	se pya póli ménete?
In..., it's near... _____	Σε...Είναι κοντά σε...
	se...íne kondá se
Have you been here _____	Είστε πολύ καιρό εδώ;
long?	*íste polí keró edhó?*
A few days _____	Μερικές μέρες
	merikés méres
How long are you _____	Πόσο καιρό θα μείνετε εδώ;
staying here?	*póso kyeró tha mínete edhó?*
We're (probably) leaving ___	(Μάλλον) θα φύγουμε αύριο/σε δύο
tomorrow/in two weeks	εβδομάδες
	(málon) tha fíghoome ávrio/se dhío
	evdhomádhes
Where are you staying? ____	Που μένετε;
	poo ménete?
In a hotel/an apartment ____	Σ' ένα ξενοδοχείο/σε διαμέρισμα
	séna xenodhohío/se dhiamérizma
On a camp site _____	Σ' ένα κάμπινγκ
	séna kámping
With friends/relatives _____	Σε φίλους/σε συγγενείς
	se fíloos/se singenís
Are you here on your _____	Είστε μόνος σας /μόνη σας /με την
own/with your family?	οικόγενειά σας;
	íste mónos sas/móni sas/me tin
	ikoyényásas?

I'm on my own_____	Είμαι μόνος μου /μόνη μου
	íme mónos moo/móni moo
I'm with my_____ partner/wife/husband	Είμαι με το /τη σύντροφό μου/τη γυναίκα μου/τον άντρα μου
	íme me to/ti síndtrofómoo/ti yinéka moo/ton ándra moo
– with my family _____	Είμαι με την οικογένειά μου
	íme me tin ikoyényámoo
– with relatives_____	Είμαι με συγγενείς μου
	íme me singenís moo
– with a friend/friends _____	Είμαι μ' ένα φίλο/με μία φίλη/με φίλους
	íme ména fílo/me mya fíli/me fíloos
Are you married? _____	Είστε παντρεμένος/παντρεμένη;
	íste pandreménos/pandreméni?
Do you have a steady _____ boyfriend/girlfriend?	Εχεις ένα φίλο/μια φιλενάδα;
	éhis éna fílo/mya filenádha?
That's none of your_____ business	Δε σας ενδιαφέρει/Δε σας πέφτει λόγος
	dhe sas endhiaféri/dhe sas péfti lóghos
I'm married _____	Είμαι παντρεμένος/παντρεμένη
	íme pandreménos/pandreméni
– single_____	Είμαι εργένης
	íme eryénis
– separated _____	Είμαι χωρισμένος/χωρισμένη (από κλίνη και στέγη)
	íme chorizménos/chorizméni (apó klíni ke stéyi)
– divorced _____	Είμαι διεζευγμένος/διεζευγμένη
	íme dhiezevghménos/dhiezevghméni
– a widow/widower_____	Είμαι χήρα/χήρος
	íme híra/híros
I live alone/with _____ someone	Μένω μόνος μου/μόνη μου/μαζί με το φίλο μου/τη φιλενάδα μου
	méno mónos moo/móni moo/mazí me to fílo moo/ti filenádha moo
Do you have any _____ children/grandchildren?	Εχετε παιδιά/εγγόνια;
	éhete pedhyá/engónya?
How old are you? _____	Πόσων χρονών είστε;
	póson chronón íste?
How old is she/he? _____	Πόσων χρονών είναι;
	póson chronón íne?
I'm... _____	Είμαι...χρονών
	íme...chronón
She's/he's... _____	Είναι...χρονών
	íne...chronón
What do you do for a _____ living?	Τί δουλειά κάνετε;
	ti dhoolyá kánete?
I work in an office _____	Δουλεύω σ' ένα γραφείο
	dhoolévo séna ghrafío
I'm a student/ _____ I'm at school	Σπουδάζω/πηγαίνω σχολείο
	spoodházo/piyéno scholío
I'm unemployed_____	Είμαι άνεργος/άνεργη
	íme ánerghos/áneryi
I'm retired _____	Είμαι συνταξιούχος/συνταξιούχα
	íme sintaxióochos/sintaxióocha
I'm on a disability _____ pension	Είμαι ανίκανος/ανίκανη για εργασία, έχω επίδομα ανικανότητας
	íme aníkanos/aníkani ya erghasía, ého epídhoma anikanótitas

Conversation

I'm a housewife	Είμαι νοικοκυρά
	íme nikokirá
Do you like your job?	Σας αρέσει η δουλειά σας;
	sas arési i dhoolyásas?
Most of the time	Μερικές φορές ναι, μερικές φορές όχι
	merikés forés ne, merikés forés óhi
I usually do, but I prefer holidays	Συνήθως μ' αρέσει, αλλά οι διακοπές μ' αρέσουν πιο πολύ
	siníthos marési, alá i dhiakopés marésoon pyo polí

3.3 Starting/ending a conversation

Could I ask you something?	Μπορώ να σας ρωτήσω κάτι;
	boró na sas rotíso káti?
Excuse me	Με συγχωρείτε
	me sinchoríte
Excuse me, could you help me?	Συγγνώμη, μήπως μπορείτε να με βοηθήσετε;
	signómi, mípos boríte na me voithísete?
Yes, what's the problem?	Ναι, ποιό είναι το πρόβλημά σας;
	ne, pyo íne to próvlimásas?
What can I do for you?	Τί μπορώ να κάνω για σας;
	ti boró na káno ya sas?
Sorry, I don't have time now	Λυπάμαι, δεν έχω καιρό τώρα
	lipáme, dhen écho keró tóra
Do you have a light?	Μήπως έχετε φωτιά;
	mípos éhete fotyá?
May I join you?	Μπορώ να καθίσω δίπλα σας;
	boró na kathíso dhípla sas?
Could you take a picture of me/us? Press this button	Μπορείτε να με/μας βγάλετε μια φωτογραφία; Να πιέστε αυτό το κουμπί
	boríte na me/mas vghálete mya fotografía? na pyéste avtó to koobí
Leave me alone	Άσε με ήσυχο
	áse me ísicho
Get lost	Εξαφανίσου
	exafanísoo
Go away or I'll scream	Αν δε φύγετε, θα βάλω τις φωνές
	an dhe fíyete, tha válo tis fonés

3.4 Congratulations and condolences

Happy birthday/many happy returns	Χρόνια πολλά
	chrónya polá
Please accept my condolences	Τα συλλυπητήριά μου
	ta silipitíryámoo
I'm very sorry for you	Ήταν μεγάλο πλήγμα
	ítan meghálo plíghma

3.5 A chat about the weather

See also 1.5 The weather

It's so hot/cold today!	Τί ζέστη/κρύο που κάνει σήμερα!
	ti zésti/krío poo káni símera!
Nice weather, isn't it?	Τί ωραίος καιρός, ε;
	ti oréos kerós, e?

What a wind/storm! _____	Τί αέρας/θύελλα!
	ti aéras/thíela!
All that rain/snow! _____	Τί βροχή/χιόνι!
	ti vrohí/hyóni!
All that fog! _____	Τί ομίχλη!
	ti omíchli!
How long has the _____ weather been like this here?	Από πότε κάνει τέτοιον καιρό εδώ; *apó póte káni tétyo keró edhó?*
Is it always this hot/cold ___ here?	Πάντα κάνει τόση ζέστη/τόσο κρύο εδώ; *pánda káni tósi zésti/tóso krío edhó?*
Is it always this dry/wet____ here?	Εχει πάντα εδώ τόση ξηρασία/υγρασία; *éhi pánda edhó tósi xirasía/ighrasía?*

🄷 .6 Hobbies

Do you have any _____ hobbies?	Εχετε χόμπυ; *éhete hóbi?*
I like painting/_____ reading/photography/	Μ' αρέσει να πλέκω/να διαβάζω/η φωτογραφία *marési na pléko/na dhiavázo/i fotoghrafía*
I like music _____	Αγαπώ τη μουσική *aghapó ti moosikí*
I like playing the _____ guitar/piano	Μ' αρέσει να παίζω κιθάρα/πιάνο *marési na pézo kithára/pyáno*
I like going to the _____ movies	Μ' αρέσει να πηγαίνω στον κινηματογράφο *marési na piyéno stonginimatoghráfo*
I like travelling/_____ sport/fishing/walking	Μ' αρέσει να ταξιδεύω/να κάνω σπορ/να ψαρεύω/να πηγαίνω περίπατο *marési na taxidhévo/na káno spor/na psarévo/na piyéno perípato*

🄷 .7 Being the host(ess)

See also 4 Eating out

Can I offer you a drink? ____	Μπορώ να σας προσφέρω ένα ποτό; *boró na sas prosféro éna potó?*
What would you like_____ to drink?	Τί θέλεις να πιεις; *ti thélis na pyis?*
Would you like a _____ cigarette/cigar/to roll your own?	Θέλετε ένα τσιγάρο/ένα πόορο/να στρίψετε ένα τσιγάρο; *thélete éna tsigháro/éna póoro/na strípsete éna tsigháro*
Something non-_____ alcoholic, please	Θα ήθελα ένα ποτό χωρίς αλκόόλ/ένα αναψυκτικό *tha íthela éna potó chorís alkól/éna anapsiktikó*
I don't smoke _____	Δεν καπνίζω *dhen kapnízo*

🄷 .8 Invitations

Are you doing anything____ tonight?	Είσαι ελεύθερος/ελεύθερη απόψε; *íse eléftheros/eléftheri apópse?*
Do you have any plans ____ for today/this afternoon/tonight?	Εχετε κανένα πρόγραμμα για σήμερα/για το απόγευμα/για απόψε; *éhete kanéna próghrama ya símera/ya to apóyevma/ya apópse?*

29

Would you like to go ___ out with me?	Θα θέλατε να βγούμε έξω μαζί; *tha thélate na vghóome éxo mazí?*
Would you like to go ___ dancing with me?	Θα θέλατε να πάμε να χορέψουμε μαζί; *tha thélate na páme na chorépsoome mazí?*
Would you like to have ___ lunch/dinner with me?	Θα θέλατε να πάμε να φάμε μαζί; *tha thélate na páme na fáme mazí?*
Would you like to come___ to the beach with me?	Θα θέλατε να πάμε μαζί στην παραλία; *tha thélate na páme mazí stimbaralía?*
Would you like to come___ into town with us?	Θα θέλατε να' ρθείτε μαζί μας στην πόλη; *tha thélate narthíte mazí mas stimbóli?*
Would you like to come___ and see some friends with us?	Θα θέλατε να' ρθείτε μαζί μας σε φίλους μας; *tha thélate narthíte mazí mas se fíloos mas?*
Shall we dance? ___	Πάμε να χορέψουμε; *páme na chorépsoome?*
– sit at the bar? ___	Πάμε να καθίσουμε στο μπαρ; *páme na kathísoome sto bar?*
– get something to drink? __	Πάμε να πιούμε κάτι; *páme na pyóome káti?*
– go for a walk/drive? ___	Πάμε να κάνουμε μια βόλτα/μια βόλτα με το αυτοκίνητο; *páme na kánoome mya vólta/mya vólta me to aftokínito*
Yes, all right ___	Ναι, εντάξει *ne, endáxi*
Good idea ___	Καλή ιδέα *kalí idhéa*
No (thank you) ___	Οχι, (ευχαριστώ) *óhi (efcharistó)*
Maybe later ___	Ισως αργότερα *ísos arghótera*
I don't feel like it ___	Δεν έχω όρεξη *dhen écho órexi*
I don't have time ___	Δεν έχω καιρό *dhen écho keró*
I already have a date ___	Εχω ένα άλλο ραντεβού *écho éna álo randevóo*
I'm not very good at___ dancing/volleyball/ swimming	Δεν ξέρω να χορεύω/να παίζω βόλλευ/να κολυμπώ *dhen xéro na chorévo/na pézo vóllei/na kolimbó*

⓷.9 Paying a compliment

You look wonderful! ___	Είστε μια χαρά! *íste mya chará!*
I like your car! ___	Τί ωραίο αυτοκίνητο! *ti oréo aftokínito!*
You're a nice boy/girl ___	Είσαι πολύ καλό παιδί/κορίτσι *íse polí kaló pedhí/korítsi*
What a sweet child! ___	Τί γλυκό παιδάκι! *ti ghlikó pedháki!*
You're a wonderful ___ dancer!	Χορεύετε πολύ καλά *chorévete polí kalá*
You're a wonderful ___ cook!	Μαγειρεύετε πολύ καλά *mayirévete polí kalá*
You're a terrific soccer ___ player!	Παίζετε πολύ καλά ποδόσφαιρο *pézete polí kalá podhósfero*

.10 Chatting someone up

I like being with you _____	Μ' αρέσει να είμαι μαζί σου
	marési na íme mazí soo
I've missed you so much __	Μου έλειψες πολύ
	moo élipses polí
I dreamt about you _____	Σε είδα στ' όνειρό μου
	se ídha stoniró moo
I think about you all day ___	Δε βγαίνεις από το νου μου
	dhe vyénis apó to noo moo
You have such a sweet ____ smile	Εχεις ένα γλυκό χαμόγελο
	éhis éna ghlikó chamóyelo
You have such beautiful ___ eyes	Εχεις πολύ ωραία μάτια
	éhis polí oréa mátya
I'm in love with you _____	Είμαι ερωτευμένος/ερωτευμένη μαζί σου
	íme erotevménos/erotevméni mazí soo
I'm in love with you too __	Κι εγώ με σένα
	kyeghó me séna
I love you_____	Σ' αγαπώ
	saghapó
I love you too _____	Κι εγώ σ' αγαπώ
	kyeghó saghapó
I don't feel as strongly _____ about you	Εγώ δεν έχω τέτοια σοβαρά αισθήματα για σένα
	eghó dhen écho tétya sovará esthímata ya séna
I already have a _____ boyfriend/girlfriend	Εχω ήδη φίλο/φιλενάδα
	écho ídhi fílo/filenádha
I'm not ready for that_____	Δεν είμαι έτοιμος/έτοιμη γι' αυτό
	dhen íme étimos/étimi yaftó
This is going too fast _____ for me	Καλύτερα να μη βιαζόμαστε τόσο
	kalítera na mi viazómaste tóso
Take your hands off me____	Μη μ' αγγίζεις
	mi mangízis
Okay, no problem _____	Εντάξει, δεν πειράζει
	endáxi, dhembirázi
Will you stay with me _____ tonight?	Θα μείνεις μαζί μου τη νύχτα;
	tha mínis mazí moo ti níchta
I'd like to go to bed_____ with you	Θέλω να κάνουμε έρωτα
	thélo na kánoome érota
Only if we use a condom __	Μόνο με προφυλακτικό
	móno me profilaktikó
We have to be careful _____ about AIDS	Πρέπει να προσέχουμε λόγω του ΕΙΤΖ
	prépi na proséchoome lógho too AIDS
That's what they all say____	Ολοι τα ίδια λένε
	óli ta ídhya léne
We shouldn't take any _____ risks	Ας μη το διακινδυνέψουμε
	mi to dhiakindhinépsoome
Do you have a condom? ___	Εχεις προφυλακτικό;
	éhis profilaktikó?
No? In that case we _____ won't do it	Οχι; Τότε δε γίνεται
	óhi? tóte dhe yínete

Conversation

3.11 Arrangements

When will I see you again?	Πότε θα σε ξαναδώ; *póte tha se xanadhó?*
Are you free over the weekend?	Θα έχετε καιρό το Σαββατοκύριακο; *tha éhete keró to savatokíriako?*
What shall we arrange?	Τί θα κανονίσουμε; *ti tha kanonísoome?*
Where shall we meet?	Πού θα συναντηθούμε; *poo tha sinandithóome?*
Will you pick me/us up?	Θα 'ρθείτε να με/μας πάρετε; *tharthíte na me/mas párete?*
Shall I pick you up?	Να περάσω να σας πάρω; *na peráso na sas páro?*
I have to be home by...	Πρέπει να είμαι σπίτι στις... *prépi na íme spíti stis...*
Can I take you home?	Μπορώ να σας πάω σπίτι; *boró na sas páo spíti?*
I don't want to see you anymore	Δε θέλω να σας ξαναδώ *dhe thélo na sas xanadhó*

3.12 Saying goodbye

Can I write/call you?	Μπορώ να σας γράψω/τηλεφωνήσω; *boró na sas ghrápso/tilefoníso?*
Will you write/call me?	Θα μου γράψετε/τηλεφωνήσετε; *tha moo ghrápsete/tilefonísete?*
Can I have your address/phone number?	Μπορώ να έχω τη διεύθυνση σας/τον αριθμό του τηλεφώνου σας; *boró na écho ti dhiésthinsi sas/ton arithmó too tilefónoo sas?*
Thanks for everything	Ευχαριστώ για όλα *efcharistó ya óla*
It was very nice	Ήταν πολύ ωραία *ítan polí oréa*
Say hello to...	Χαιρετισμούς σε *heretizmóos se...*
All the best	Σου εύχομαι ό,τι καλύτερο *soo éfchome óti kalítero*
Good luck	Καλή επιτυχία στο μέλλον *kalí epitihía sto mélon*
When will you be back?	Πότε θα ξαναέρθεις; *póte tha xanaérthis?*
I'll be waiting for you	Θα σε περιμένω *tha se periméno*
I'd like to see you again	Θα ήθελα πολύ να σε ξαναδώ *tha íthela polí na se xanadhó*
I hope we meet again soon	Ελπίζω να ξαναιδωθούμε σύντομα *elpízo na xanaidhothóome síndoma*
This is our address. If you're ever in the UK...	Αυτή είναι η διεύθυνσή μας. Αν κάποτε βρεθείτε στο Ηνωμένο Βασίλειο... *aftí íne i dhiéfthinsí mas. an kápote vrethíte sto inoméno vasilío...*
You'd be more than welcome	Είστε πάντα ευπρόσδεκτος/ευπρόσδεκτη *íste pánda efprósdhektos/efprósdhekti*

Eating out

4 Eating out

● **In Greece** people usually have three meals:
1 *το πρωινό* (breakfast), between 7.00 and 10 am. Breakfast is
light and consists of a cup of coffee with bread and jam or honey.
2 *το γεύμα* (lunch), between 1.00 and 3.00pm. Lunch always
includes a hot dish and is the most important meal of the day.
3 *το δείπνο* (dinner), between 9.00pm and 1.00am. Dinner is a hot meal
similar to lunch though a little lighter. It is usually taken with the family.

4 .1 On arrival

I'd like to book a table _____ for seven o'clock, please	Μπορώ να κλείσω ένα τραπέζι γι' απόψε στις εφτά;
	boró na klíso éna trapézi yapópse stis eftá?
I'd like a table for two, _____ please	Θα ήθελα ένα τραπέζι για δύο άτομα
	tha íthela éna trapézi ya dhío átoma
We've/we haven't booked __	(Δεν) κλείσαμε τραπέζι
	(dhen) klísame trapézi
Is the restaurant open _____ yet?	Είναι ανοιχτή η κουζίνα;
	íne anichtí i koozína?
What time does the _____ restaurant open/close?	Πότε ανοίγει/κλείνει η κουζίνα;
	póte aníyi/klíni i koozína?
Can we wait for a table? ___	Μπορούμε να περιμένουμε για ένα τραπέζι;
	boróome na periménoome ya éna trapézi?
Will we have to _____ wait long?	Θα πρέπει να περιμένουμε πολλή ώρα;
	tha prépi na periménoome polí óra?
Is this seat taken? _____	Είναι ελεύθερη αυτή η θέση;
	íne eléftheri aftí i thési?
Could we sit here/there? ___	Μπορούμε να καθίσουμε εδώ/εκεί;
	boróome na kathísoome edhó/ekí?
Can we sit by the_____ window?	Μπορούμε να καθίσουμε κοντά στο παράθυρο;
	boróome na kathísoome kondá sto paráthiro?
Can we eat outside? _____	Μπορούμε να φάμε κι έξω;
	boróome na fáme kyéxo?
Do you have another _____ chair for us?	Μας φέρνετε ακόμα μια καρέκλα;
	mas férnete akóma mya karékla?
Do you have a highchair? __	Μας φέρνετε μια παιδική καρέκλα;
	mas férnete mya pedhikí karékla?
Is there a socket for _____ this bottle-warmer?	Υπάρχει μια πρίζα γι' αυτό το βραστήρα;
	ipárhi mya príza yavtó to vrastíra?

Κλείσατε τραπέζι; _____	Do you have a reservation?
Με ποιό όνομα;_____	What name, please?
Από δω, παρακαλώ _____	This way, please
Αυτό το τραπέζι είναι κλεισμένο_____	This table is reserved
Σ' ένα τέταρτο θά 'χουμε ελεύθερο _____ τραπέζι	We'll have a table free in fifteen minutes
Μπορείτε να περιμένετε στο (μπαρ); ___	Would you like to wait (at the bar)?

Could you warm up _____ this bottle/jar for me?	Μπορείτε να μου ζεστάνετε αυτό το μπιμπερό/βαζάκι; *boríte na moo zestánete avtó to biberó/vazáki?*
Not too hot, please _____	Να μην είναι πολύ ζεστό, παρακαλώ *na min íne polí zestó, parakaló*
Is there somewhere I _____ can change the baby's nappy?	Υπάρχει κάποιος χώρος όπου μπορώ να αλλάξω το μωρό; *ipárhi kápyos chóros ópoo boró na aláxo to moró?*
Where are the toilets? _____	Πού είναι η τουαλέτα; *poo íne i twaléta?*

4.2 Ordering

Waiter!/Madam!/Sir!_____	Γκαρσόνι!/Κυρία/Κύριε! *garsóni!/kiría!/kírie!*
We'd like something to _____ eat/a drink	Θέλουμε να φάμε/να πιούμε κάτι *théloome na fáme/na pyóome káti*
Could I have a quick _____ meal?	Μπορώ να φάω κάτι γρήγορα; *boró na fáo káti ghrígora?*
We don't have much _____ time	Βιαζόμαστε *viazomaste*
We'd like to have a _____ drink first	Θέλουμε πρώτα να πιούμε κάτι *théloome próta na pyóome káti*
Could we see the_____ menu/wine list, please?	Μπορούμε να δούμε τον κατάλογο/τον κατάλογο κρασιών; *boróome na dhóome tongatálogho/tongatálogho krasyón?*
Do you have a menu _____ in English?	Εχετε ένα κατάλογο στα αγγλικά; *éhete éna katálogho sta angliká?*
Do you have a dish_____ of the day?/Do you have a tourist menu?	Εχετε πιάτο της ημέρας/τουριστικό μενού; *éhete pyáto tis iméras/tooristikó menóo?*
We haven't made a_____ choice yet	Δεν αποφασίσαμε ακόμα *dhen apofasísame akóma*
What do you _____ recommend?	Τί μπορείτε να μας προτείνετε; *ti boríte na mas protínete?*
What are the specialities_____ of the region/the house?	Ποιές είναι οι σπεσιαλιτέ της περιοχής/του μαγαζιού; *pyes íne i spesialité tis periohís/too maghazyóo?*
I like strawberries/olives _____	Μ' αρέσουν οι φράουλες/οι ελιές *marésoon i fráooles/i elyés*
I don't like fish/meat... _____	Δε μ' αρέσει το ψάρι/το κρέας/... *dhe marési to psári/to kréas/...*
What's this?_____	Τί είναι αυτό; *ti íne aftó?*
Does it have...in it? _____	Εχει μέσα...; *éhi mésa...?*
What does it taste like? _____	Με τί μοιάζει; *me ti myázi?*
Is this a hot or a_____ cold dish?	Αυτό το φαγητό είναι κρύο ή ζεστό; *aftó to fayitó íne krío i zestó?*
Is this sweet? _____	Αυτό το φαγητό είναι γλυκό; *aftó to fayitó íne ghlikó?*

Eating out

Is this spicy/hot? _____	Αυτό το φαγητό είναι πικάντικο/πιπεράτο;
	aftó to fayitó íne pikándiko/piperáto?
Do you have _____ anything else?	Μήπως έχετε κάτι άλλο;
	mípos éhete káti álo?
I'm on a salt-free diet _____	Απαγορεύεται να τρώω αλάτι
	apaghorévete na tró-o aláti
I can't eat pork _____	Απαγορεύεται να τρώω χοιρινό κρέας
	apaghorévete na tró-o hirinó kréas
– sugar _____	Απαγορεύεται να τρώω ζάχαρη
	apaghorévete na tró-o záchari
– fatty foods _____	Απαγορεύεται να τρώω λίπη
	apaghorévete na tró-o lípi
– (hot) spices _____	Απαγορεύεται να τρώω (καυτερά) μπαχαρικά
	apaghorévete na tró-o (kafterá) bachariká
I'll/we'll have what those___ people are having	Θέλουμε το ίδιο φαγητό που τρώνε εκείνοι οι άνθρωποι, παρακαλώ
	théloome to ídhyo fayitó poo tróne ekíni i ánthropi, parakaló
I'd like... _____	Θα ήθελα...
	tha íthela ...
We're not having a _____ starter	Δε θέλουμε ορεκτικό
	dhe théloome orektikó
The child will share what __ we're having	Το παιδί θα φάει λίγο από το δικό μας φαγητό
	to pedhí tha fái lígho apó to dhikó mas fayitó
Could I have some _____ more bread, please?	Παρακαλώ, λίγο ψωμί ακόμα
	parakaló, lígho psomí akóma
– a bottle of water/wine____	Παρακαλώ, ένα μπουκάλι νερό/κρασί ακόμα
	parakaló, éna bookáli neró/krasí akóma
– another helping of... _____	Παρακαλώ, μια μερίδα... ακόμα
	parakaló, mya merídha ... akóma
– some salt and pepper ____	Μας φέρνετε το αλατοπίπερο, παρακαλώ;
	mas férnete to alatopípero, parakaló?
– a napkin _____	Μας φέρνετε μια χαρτοπετσέτα, παρακαλώ;
	mas férnete mya chartopetséta, parakaló
– a spoon_____	Μας φέρνετε ένα κουταλάκι, παρακαλώ;
	mas férnete éna kootaláki, parakaló?
– an ashtray _____	Μας φέρνετε ένα τασάκι, παρακαλώ;
	mas férnete éna tasáki, parakaló?
– some matches_____	Μας φέρνετε σπίρτα, παρακαλώ;
	mas férnete spírta, parakaló?
– some toothpicks_____	Μας φέρνετε οδοντογλυφίδες, παρακαλώ;
	mas férnete odhondoghlifídhes, parakaló?
– a glass of water _____	Μας φέρνετε ένα ποτήρι νερό, παρακαλώ;
	mas férnete éna potíri neró, parakaló?
– a straw (for the child) ____	Μας φέρνετε ένα καλαμάκι (για το παιδί), παρακαλώ;
	mas férnete éna kalamáki (ya to pédhi), parakaló?
Enjoy your meal!_____	Καλή όρεξη!
	kalí órexi!

Θέλετε να φάτε; _____	Do you want to eat?
Διαλέξατε τί θέλετε να φάτε; _____	Have you decided what you want?
Θέλετε ένα απεριτίφ; _____	Would you like a drink first?
Τί θέλετε να πιείτε; _____	What would you like to drink?
Καλή όρεξη _____	Enjoy your meal
Θέλετε ένα γλυκό/ένα καφέ; _____	Would you like a dessert/coffee?

You too! _____	Επίσης *epísis*
Cheers! _____	Στην υγειά σας! *stin iyá sas!*
The next round's on me ___	Το επόμενο κέρασμα είναι δικό μου *to epómeno kyérazma íne dhikó moo*
Could we have a doggy____ bag, please?	Μπορούμε να πάρουμε τ' απομεινάρια για το σκύλο μας; *boróome na pároome tapominária ya to skílo mas?*

4 .3 The bill

See also 8.2 Settling the bill

How much is this dish? ____	Πόσο κάνει αυτό το φαγητό; *póso káni aftó to fayitó?*
Could I have the bill, _____ please?	Το λογαριασμό, παρακαλώ *to loghariazmó, parakaló*
All together _____	Ολα μαζί *óla mazí*
Everyone pays separately ___	Ο καθένας πληρόνει τα δικά του *o kathénas pliróni ta dhiká too*
Could we have the menu ___ again, please?	Μπορούμε να ξαναδούμε τον κατάλογο; *boróome na xanadhóome tongatálogho?*
The...is not on the bill _____	Το...δεν είναι στο λογαριασμό *to...dhen íne sto loghariazmó*

4 .4 Complaints

It's taking a very_____ long time	Αργείτε πολύ *aryíte polí*
We've been here an _____ hour already	Περιμένουμε ήδη μια ώρα *periménoome ídhi mya óra*
This must be a mistake ____	Πρέπει να έγινε κάποιο λάθος *prépi na éyine kápyo láthos*
This is not what I_____ ordered	Δεν παράγγειλα αυτό *dhen parángila aftó*
I ordered..._____	Παράγγειλα... *parángila...*
There's a dish missing_____	Λείπει ένα φαγητό *lípi éna fayitó*

This is broken/not clean ___	Αυτό είναι σπασμένο/δεν είναι καθαρό
	aftó íne spazméno/dhen íne katharó
The food's cold _____	Το φαγητό είναι κρύο
	to fayitó íne krío
– not fresh _____	Το φαγητό δεν είναι φρέσκο
	to fayitó dhen íne frésko
– too salty/sweet/spicy ____	Το φαγητό είναι πολύ αλμυρό/γλυκό/πικάντικο
	to fayitó íne polí almiró/ghlikó/pikándiko
The meat's not done_____	Το κρέας δεν είναι ψημένο
	to kréas dhen íne psiméno
– overdone _____	Το κρέας είναι πολύ ψημένο
	to kréas íne polí psiméno
– tough _____	Το κρέας είναι σκληρό
	to kréas íne skliró
– off_____	Το κρέας είναι χαλασμένο
	to kréas íne chalazméno
Could I have something ___ else instead of this?	Μπορείτε να μου δώσετε κάτι άλλο;
	boríte na moo dhósete káti álo?
The bill/this amount is _____ not right	Ο λογαριασμός/αυτό το ποσό δεν είναι σωστός/σωστό
	o loghariazmós/aftó to posó dhen íne sostós/sostó
We didn't have this_____	Αυτό δεν το είχαμε
	aftó dhen to íchame
There's no paper in the ____ toilet	Δεν έχει χαρτί στην τουαλέτα
	dhen éhi chartí stin twaléta
Do you have a _____ complaints book?	Εχετε βιβλίο παραπόνων;
	éhete vivlío parapónon?
Will you call the_____ manager, please?	Φωνάξτε το αφεντικό σας, παρακαλώ
	fonáxte to afendikósas, parakaló

4.5 Paying a compliment

That was a wonderful _____ meal	Φάγαμε πολύ καλά
	fághame polí kalá
The food was excellent ____	Ηταν πολύ νόστιμο
	ítan polí nóstimo
The...in particular was _____ delicious	Προπαντός το...ήταν εξαιρετικό
	propandós to...ítan exeretikó

αλκοολούχα ποτά
alcoholic beverages
απεριτίφ
aperitif
επιδόρπια
dessert
ζεστά φαγητά
hot dishes
θαλασσινά
seafood
κατά προτίμηση
prepared as you want it
κατάλογος κρασιών
wine list
κρέας
meat
κρύα φαγητά
cold dishes

λαχανικά
vegetables
μεζέδες
mixed starters (also
  used when drinking
  ouzo)
ντόπια φαγητά
local dishes
ορεκτικά
appetisers
πάστες
cakes/pastries
πιάτα της ημέρας
dish of the day
πουλερικά
poultry
πρωινό
breakfast

σούπες
soups
σπεσιαλιτέ
speciality
συμπεριλαμβανομένης
  υπηρεσίας
service included
της σχάρας
grilled dishes
της ώρας
prepared while you wait
Φ.Π.Α.
VAT
φαγητά για
  χορτοφάγους
vegetarian dishes
ψάρι
fish

αγγούρι
cucumber
αγκινάρες
globe artichokes
αλάτι
salt
αμύγδαλο (-λα)
almond (s)
αντίδια
endives
αντσούγιες
anchovies
αρακάς
peas
αρνί/αρνίσιο κρέα
lamb
αστακός
lobster
αυγά μάτι
fried eggs
αυγολέμονο
egg and lemon
  (sauce or soup)
αχλάδι(α)
pear(s)
βασιλόπιτα
New Year's cake
βατόμουρα
blackberries

βερύκοκα
apricots
βοδινό κρέας
beef
βούτυρο
butter
βραστό
boiled
βυσσινάδα
sour cherry
drink
γάλα
milk
γαλακτομπούρεκο
cake made with
  filo pastry
  and confectioner's
  custard
γαλλόπουλο
turkey
γαρίδες
prawns
γεμιστό
stuffed
γιαούρτι
yoghurt
γιαχνί
a stew

γίγαντες
large white beans
γιουβαρλάκια
meatballs
γιουβέτσι
a form of pasta
γλώσσα
sole (fish)
γραβιέρα
cheese
γρανίτα
a drink made
  with crushed ice
  and fruit
δαμάσκηνο (-να)
plums/prunes
δάφνη
bayleaf
ελιές
olives
ζαμπόν
ham
ζάχαρη
sugar
ζουμί
broth
θυμάρι
thyme

Eating out

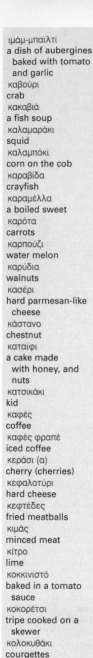

ιμάμ-μπαιλτί
a dish of aubergines baked with tomato and garlic

καβούρι
crab

κακαβιά
a fish soup

καλαμαράκι
squid

καλαμπόκι
corn on the cob

καραβίδα
crayfish

καραμέλλα
a boiled sweet

καρότα
carrots

καρπούζι
water melon

καρύδια
walnuts

κασέρι
hard parmesan-like cheese

κάστανο
chestnut

καταΐφι
a cake made with honey, and nuts

κατσικάκι
kid

καφές
coffee

καφές φραπέ
iced coffee

κεράσι (α)
cherry (cherries)

κεφαλοτύρι
hard cheese

κεφτέδες
fried meatballs

κιμάς
minced meat

κίτρο
lime

κοκκινιστό
baked in a tomato sauce

κοκορέτσι
tripe cooked on a skewer

κολοκυθάκι
courgettes

κολοκύθι
marrow/pumpkin

κομπόστα
compote

κοτόπουλο
chicken

κουκιά
broad beans

κουλουράκι (α)
small ring-shaped biscuits

κουλούρι
hard ring-shaped sesame bread

κουνέλι
rabbit

κουραμπιέδες
cakes made with almonds and caster sugar

κρασί
wine

κρέας
meat

κρέμα
confectioner's custard

κρεμμύδι(α)
onion(s)

κυνήγι
game

λαγός
hare

λάδι
oil

λαχανάκια Βρυξελλών
Brussels sprouts

λαχανικό (-κά)
vegetable(s)

λάχανο
cabbage

λεμονάδα
lemonade

λεμόνι
lemon

λουκάνικα
sausages

λουκουμάδες
light doughnuts served with spiced honey

λουκούμι
Turkish Delight

μαγειρίτσα
an Easter soup made from lamb and goat entrails

μαϊντανό
parsley

μανιτάρι
mushrooms

μανούρι
a white cheese

μαρίδες
whitebait

μαρμελάδα
jam

μαρούλι
lettuce

μέλι
honey

μελιτζάνα
aubergine

μελομακάρονα
cakes made of honey and nuts

μήλο
apple

μιζήθρα
a soft goat's cheese

μοσχάρι/μοσχαρίσιο κρέας
veal

μοσχοκάρυδο
nutmeg

μούρο
mulberry

μουσακάς
a dish made with layers of minced lamb and aubergine

μούσμουλα
loquat

μουστάρδα
mustard

μπακαλιάρος
dried cod

μπακλαβάς
cake made with filo pastry, nuts and honey

μπάμιες
okra

μπαρμπούνι
red mullet

μπιζέλια
peas

μπιφτέκι
burger

μπουγάτσα
a cake made with
  filo pastry and
  confectioner's
  custard
μπούτι
thigh
μπριζόλα βοδινή
beef chop/cutlet
μπύρα
beer
μυαλά
brains
μύδια
mussels
νερό
water
νεφρά
kidneys
ντολμάδες
stuffed vine-leaves
ντομάτες
tomatoes
ντομάτες
  γεμιστές
stuffed tomatoes
ξηροί καρποί
dried fruit
ξίδι/ξύδι
vinegar
ομελέτα
omelette
ούζο
ouzo (aniseed-
  flavoured spirit)
ουίσκυ
whiskey
παγωτό
ice cream
παϊδάκι
lamb chop
παντζάρια
beetroots
πάπια
duck
παπουτσάκια
stuffed aubergines
πάστες
cakes
παστίτσιο
minced meat and
  macaroni pie
παστό
salted
πατάτες
potatoes

πατσάς
soup made from
  tripe
πεπόνι
melon
πέστροφα
trout
πετεινάρι κρασάτο
coq au vin
πιλάφι
pilaff rice
πιπέρι
pepper
πιπεριά
green or red pepper
  (vegetable)
πιτσούνι
young pigeons
πλάτη
shoulder
πορτοκαλάδα
orange
  juice/orangeade
πορτοκάλι
orange
πράσο
leek
ραδίκια
chicory
ραπανάκια
radishes
ρεβύθια
chick-peas
ρέγγα
herring (smoked)
ρετσίνα
wine flavoured with
  pine resin
ρίγανη
oregano
ροδάκινο
peach
ρόδι
pomegranate
ρύζι
rice
ρυζόγαλο
rice pudding
σαλάτα
salad
σαλιγγάρια
snails
σάλτσα
sauce
σαντιγί
whipped cream

σάντουιτς
sandwich
σαρδέλλες
sardines
σέλινο
celery
σκορδαλιά
dip made from garlic
  and bread or
  potato
σκόρδο
garlic
σκουμπρί
mackerel
σοκολάτα
chocolate
σολομός
salmon
σουβλάκι
grilled meat on a
  skewer
σούπα
soup
σουπιές
cuttle fish
σουτζουκάκια
spicy meat-balls in
  tomato sauce
σπανάκι
spinach
στα κάρβουνα
barbecued
σταφίδα
raisin
σταφύλια
grapes
στη σχάρα
on the grill
στιφάδο
stew made with
  shallots and
  flavoured with
  sweet wine
στο φούρνο
cooked in the oven
στρείδι
oysters
σύκα
figs
συκώτι
liver
σφυρίδα
grey mullet
ταραμάς
smoked cod's roe

41

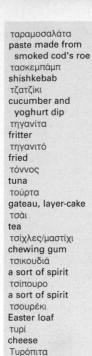

ταραμοσαλάτα
paste made from
  smoked cod's roe
τασκεμπάμπ
shishkebab
τζατζίκι
cucumber and
  yoghurt dip
τηγανίτα
fritter
τηγανιτό
fried
τόννος
tuna
τούρτα
gateau, layer-cake
τσάι
tea
τσίχλες/μαστίχι
chewing gum
τσικουδιά
a sort of spirit
τσίπουρο
a sort of spirit
τσουρέκι
Easter loaf
τυρί
cheese
Τυρόπιτα
cheese pie

φασκόμηλο
aromatic herb tea
φασολάκια
green beans
φασόλια
haricot beans
φέτα
goat's cheese
φιλέτο
fillet steak
φουντούκια
hazelnuts
φράουλες
strawberries
φράπα
a variety of grapefruit
φρούτο
fruit
φρυγανιά
toast, French-style
φυστίκια
pistachio nuts
χαβιάρι
caviar
χαλβάς
a sweet made with
  semolina, honey
  and nuts
χαμομήλι
camomile

χέλι
eel
χήνα
goose
χοιρινό
pork
χόρτα
green dandelion
  leaves used in
  salad
χουρμάς
date
χταπόδι
octopus
χυμός
juice
χωριάτικη σαλάτα
a salad made
from tomatoes,
  cucumber, black
  olives and goat's
  cheese
ψάρι
fish
ψητό
roast/baked
ψωμί
bread

5

On the road

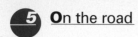

5 **O**n the road

5.1 **A**sking for directions

Excuse me, could I ask you something?	Συγγνώμη, μπορώ να σας ρωτήσω κάτι; *sighnómi, boró na sas rotíso káti?*
I've lost my way	'Εχασα το δρόμο *échasa to dhrómo*
Is there a(n)... around here?	Ξέρετε κανένα...εδώ κοντά; *xérete kanéna...edhó kondá?*
Is this the way to...?	Αυτός είναι ο δρόμος για..; *aftós íne o dhrómos ya...?*
Could you tell me how to get to... (name of place)	Μπορείτε να μου πείτε πώς μπορώ να πάω σε... ; *boríte na moo píte pos boró na páo se...?*
What's the quickest way to...?	Ποιός είναι ο πιο σύντομος δρόμος για... ; *pyos íne o pyo síndomos dhrómos ya ...?*
How many kilometres is it to...?	Πόσα χιλιόμετρα είναι ακόμα ως...; *pósa hilyómetra íne akóma os...?*
Could you point it out on the map?	Μπορείτε να το δείξετε στο χάρτη; *boríte na to díxete sto chartí?*

Δεν ξέρω, δεν είμαι από δω	I don't know, I don't know my way around here
Πήρατε λάθος δρόμο	You're going the wrong way
Πρέπει να γυρίσετε σε...	You have to go back to...
Εκεί θ' ακολουθήσετε τις πινακίδες	From there on just follow the signs
Εκεί θα ξαναρωτήσετε	When you get there, ask again

ίσια straight ahead	το φανάρι the traffic light	η γέφυρα the bridge
αριστερά left	το τούνελ the tunnel	η διάβαση του τρένου/οι μπάρες
δεξιά right	η πινακίδα διασταύρωση προτεραιότητας	the level crossing
στρίβω turn	the 'give way' sign	η πινακίδα που δείχνει το δρόμο για...
ακολουθώ follow	το κτίριο the building	the sign pointing to...
περνάω το δρόμο cross the road	στη γωνιά at the corner	το βέλος the arrow
η διασταύρωση the intersection	το ποτάμι the river	
ο δρόμος/η οδός the street	η ανισόπεδη διασταύρωση the flyover	

5.2 Customs

● **Border documents:** valid passport. For car and motorbike: valid UK driving licence and registration document, insurance document, green card, UK registration plate. Caravan: must be entered on the green card and driven with the same registration number. A warning triangle, headlamp converters and extra headlamp bulbs should be carried. Insurance should also be upgraded.

Import and export specifications:

Foreign currency: a maximum of 100,000 drachmas may be taken into the country, and a maximum of 20,000 may be taken out.

Alcohol (aged 18 and above): 1 and a half litres of spirits, fortified or sparkling wine. Tobacco (aged 17 and above): 300 cigarettes or 150 cigars or 400 grams of tobacco.

Το διαβατήριό σας, παρακαλώ _____	Your passport, please
Την πράσινη κάρτα σας, παρακαλώ _____	Your green card, please
Τον αριθμό κυκλοφορίας σας, _____ παρακαλώ	Your vehicle documents, please
Τη βίζα σας, παρακαλώ_____	Your visa, please
Πού πάτε;_____	Where are you heading?
Πόσο καιρό σκοπεύετε να μείνετε; _____	How long are you planning to stay?
Έχετε τίποτα να δηλώσετε; _____	Do you have anything to declare?
Ανοίξτε αυτό, παρακαλώ _____	Open this, please

My children are entered ___ on this passport	Τα παιδιά μου είναι γραμμένα σ' αυτό το διαβατήριο *ta pedhyámoo íne ghraména saftó to dhiavatírio*
I'm travelling through _____	Είμαι περαστικός/περαστική *íme perastikós/perastikí*
I'm going on holiday to... __	Πηγαίνω για διακοπές σε... *piyéno ya dhiakopés se*
I'm on a business trip _____	Είμαι εδώ για δουλειές *íme edhó ya dhoolyés*
I don't know how long_____ I'll be staying yet	Δεν ξέρω ακόμα πόσο καιρό θα μείνω *dhengxéro akóma póso kyeró tha míno*
I'll be staying here for _____ a weekend	Θα μείνω εδώ ένα Σαββατοκύριακο *tha míno edhó éna savatokíryako*
– for a few days _____	Θα μείνω εδώ λίγες μέρες *tha míno edhó líyes méres*
– for a week_____	Θα μείνω εδώ μία εβδομάδα *tha míno edhó mía evdhomádha*
– for two weeks _____	Θα μείνω εδώ δύο εβδομάδες *tha míno edhó dhío evdhomádhes*
I've got nothing to_____ declare	Δεν έχω τίποτα να δηλώσω *dhenécho típota na dhilóso*
I've got...with me_____	Έχω...μαζί μου *écho...mazímoo*

– ...cartons of cigarettes ___ Έχω μία κούτα τσιγάρα μαζί μου
écho mía kóota tsighára mazímoo

– a bottle of... _____ Έχω ένα μπουκάλι... μαζί μου
écho éna bookáli...mazímoo

– some souvenirs _____ Έχω μερικά σουβενίρ μαζί μου
écho meriká soovenír mazímoo

These are personal _____ Αυτά είναι προσωπικά αντικείμενα
effects
aftá íne prosopiká andikímena

These are not new _____ Αυτά τα πράματα δεν είναι καινούρια
aftá ta prámata dhen íne kenóorya

Here's the receipt _____ Εδώ είναι η απόδειξη
edhó íne i apódhixi

This is for private use ____ Αυτό είναι για προσωπική χρήση
aftó íne ya prosopikí chrísi

How much import duty ____ Πόσο φόρο πρέπει να πληρώσω;
do I have to pay?
póso fóro prépi na pliróso?

Can I go now? _____ Μπορώ να φύγω τώρα;
boró na fígho tóra?

5 .3 Luggage

Porter! _____ Αχθοφόρε!
achthofóre!

Could you take this_____ Παρακαλώ, πηγαίνετε αυτές τις αποσκευές σε...
luggage to...?
parakaló, piyénete aftés tis aposkevés se...

How much do I_____ Πόσο σας οφείλω;
owe you?
póso sas ofílo?

Where can I find a_____ Πού μπορώ να βρω ένα καροτσάκι;
luggage trolley?
poo boró na vro éna karotsáki?

Could you store this_____ Μπορώ να δώσω αυτές τις αποσκευές προς
luggage for me? φύλαξη;
*boró na dhóso aftés tis aposkevés pros
fílaxi?*

Where are the luggage ____ Που βρίσκονται οι θυρίδες αποσκευών;
lockers?
poo vrískonde i thirídhes aposkevón?

I can't get the locker _____ Δεν μπορώ να ανοίξω τη θυρίδα
open
dhemboró na aníxo ti thirídha

How much is it per item ___ Πόσο κοστίζει το κομμάτι/ τη μέρα;
per day?
póso kostízi to komáti/ti méra?

This is not my bag/_____ Αυτή δεν είναι δική μου τσάντα/βαλίτσα
suitcase
aftí dhen íne dhikímoo tsánda/valítsa

There's one item/bag/ _____ Λείπει ακόμα ένα κομμάτι/μια τσάντα/μια
suitcase missing still βαλίτσα
*lípi akóma éna komáti/mya tsánda/mya
valítsa*

My suitcase is damaged ___ Η βαλίτσα μου έπαθε κάποια ζημιά
i valítsa moo épathe kápya zimyá

ΑΠΑΓΟΡΕΥΕΤΑΙ Η
ΠΡΟΣΠΕΡΑΣΗ
no overtaking

ΑΠΑΓΟΡΕΥΕΤΑΙ Η
ΣΤΑΘΜΕΥΣΗ
no parking

ΑΡΓΑ
slow

ΑΥΤΟΚΙΝΗΤΟΔΡΟΜΟΣ
road suitable for cars

ΑΦΥΛΑΚΤΗ
ΔΙΑΒΑΣΗ
unmanned crossing

ΔΕΥΤΕΡΕΥΩΝ
ΔΡΟΜΟΣ
minor road

ΔΙΑΧΩΡΙΣΜΟΣ
road divides

ΔΙΟΔΙΑ
toll

ΔΩΣΕΤΕ
ΠΡΟΤΕΡΑΙΟΤΗΤΑ
give way

ΕΘΝΙΚΗ ΟΔΟΣ
(ΜΕ ΔΙΟΔΙΑ)
motorway
(with toll)

ΕΙΣΟΔΟΣ
entrance

ΕΛΑΤΤΩΣΑΤΕ
ΤΑΧΥΤΗΤΑ
reduce speed

ΕΛΕΥΘΕΡΗ
ΚΥΚΛΟΦΟΡΙΑ
clearway

ΕΠΑΡΧΙΑΚΗ ΟΔΟΣ
minor road

ΕΠΙΚΙΝΔΥΝΗ
ΔΙΑΣΤΑΥΡΩΣΗ
dangerous junction

ΕΠΙΚΙΝΔΥΝΗ
ΚΑΤΩΦΕΡΕΙΑ
steep hill

ΕΠΙΚΙΝΔΥΝΗ
ΣΤΡΟΦΗ
dangerous bend

ΕΞΟΔΟΣ
exit

ΕΞΟΔΟΣ
ΟΧΗΜΑΤΩΝ
exit for heavy
goods vehicles

Η ΤΑΧΥΤΗΤΑ
ΕΛΕΓΧΕΤΑΙ ΜΕ
ΡΑΝΤΑΡ
radar speed checks

ΚΑΤΟΛΙΣΘΗΣΕΙΣ
loose chippings

ΚΕΝΤΡΟ
centre

ΚΙΝΔΥΝΟΣ
danger

ΚΛΕΙΣΤΗ ΟΔΟΣ
road closed

ΚΥΚΛΟΦΟΡΙΑ ΑΠΟ
ΑΝΤΙΘΕΤΗ
ΚΑΤΕΥΘΥΝΣΗ
oncoming traffic

ΜΟΝΟΔΡΟΜΟΣ
one-way street

ΝΟΣΟΚΟΜΕΙΟ
hospital

ΟΔΟΣ
ΠΡΟΤΕΡΑΙΟΤΗΤΑΣ
road with priority
over vehicles
entering from side
roads

ΠΑΡΑΚΑΜΠΤΗΡΙΟΣ
diversion

ΠΕΖΟΔΡΟΜΟΣ
pavement

ΠΕΡΙΜΕΝΕΤΕ
wait

ΠΡΟΣΟΧΗ
look out!

ΠΡΟΣ ΠΑΡΑΛΙΑ
to the beach

ΣΤΑΘΜΟΣ ΠΡΩΤΩΝ
ΒΟΗΘΕΙΩΝ
first aid post

ΣΤΕΝΩΜΑ
ΟΔΟΣΤΡΩΜΑΤΟΣ
road narrows

ΣΤΡΟΦΕΣ
bends

ΤΕΛΟΣ
ΑΠΑΓΟΡΕΥΜΕΝΗΣ
ΖΩΝΗΣ
end of forbidden
zone

ΥΨΟΣ
ΠΕΡΙΟΡΙΣΜΕΝΟ
restricted height

ΧΩΜΑΤΟΔΡΟΜΟΣ
packed-earth road

The parts of a car

(the diagram shows the numbered parts)

1 battery	η μπαταρία	i bataría
2 rear light	το πίσω φως	to píso fos
3 rear-view mirror	ο καθρέφτης οδηγήσεως	o kathréftis odhiyíseos
reversing light	το πίσω φανάρι πορείας	to píso fanári porías
4 aerial	η αντένα	i anténa
car radio	το ραδιόφωνο του αυτοκινήτου	to radhiófono too aftokinítoo
5 petrol tank	το ρεζερβουάρ	to rezervwár
6 sparking plugs	το μπουζί	to boozí
fuel filter	το φίλτρο καυσίμων	to fíltro kafsímon
fuel pump	η αντλία καυσίμων	i andlía kafsímon
7 wing mirror	ο εξωτερικός καθρέφτης	o exoterikós kathréftis
8 bumper	ο προφυλακτήρας	o profilaktíras
carburettor	το καρμπυρατέρ	to karbiratér
crankcase	το κάρτερ	to kárter
cylinder	ο κύλινδρος	o kílindhros
ignition	οι πλατίνες	i platínes
warning light	η λάμπα ελέγχου	i lámpa elénchoo to
dynamo	το δυναμό	to dhinamó
accelerator	το πηδάλι γκάζι	to pidháli too gaz
handbrake	το χειρόφρενο	to hirófreno
valve	η βαλβίδα	i valvídha
9 silencer	ο σιγαστείρας	o sighastíras
10 boot	το πορτμπαγκάζ	to portbagáz
11 headlight	ο προβολέας	o provoléas
crank shaft	ο στροφαλοφόρος	o strofalofóros
12 air filter	το φίλτρο αέρος	to fíltro aéros
fog lamp	το πίσω φως ομίχλης	to píso fos omíchlis
13 engine block	το σώμα της μηχανής	to sóma tis mihanís
camshaft	ο εκκεντροφόρος άξονας	o ekendrofóros áxonas
oil filter	το φίλτρο λαδιού	to fíltro ladhyóo
oil pump	η αντλία λαδιού	i andlía ladhyóo
dipstick	ο δείκτης λαδιού	o dhíktis ladhyóo
pedal	το πηδάλι	to pidháli
14 door	η πόρτα	i pórta
15 radiator	το ψυγείο	to psiyío
16 brake disc	ο δίσκος του φρένου	o dhiskos too frénoo
spare wheel	η ρεσέρβα	i resérva
17 indicator	το φλας	to flas
18 windscreen wiper	ο γυαλοκαθαριστήρας	o yalokatharistíras
19 shock absorbers	τα αμορτισέρ	ta amortisér
sunroof	η κινητή σκεπή	i kinití skepí
starter motor	το στάρτερ	to stárter
20 steering column	η στήλη του τιμονιού	i stíli too timonyóo
21 exhaust pipe	η εξάτμιση	i exátmisi
22 seat belt	η ζώνη ασφαλείας	i zóni asfalías
fan	ο ανεμιστήρας	o anemistíras
23 distributor cables	οι αγωγοί διανομής	i aghoyí dhianomís
24 gear lever	ο λεβιές αλλαγής ταχυτήτων	io levyés alayís tahitíton

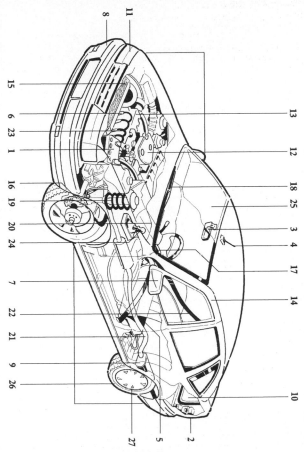

25	windscreen	το παρμπρίζ	to parbríz
	water pump	η αντλία νερού	i andlía neróo
26	wheel	η ρόδα	i ródha
27	hubcap	το καπάκι της	to kapáki tis ródhas
	piston	ρόδας	to émvolo
		το έμβολο	

 .5 The car

See the diagram on page 49.

● **Particular traffic regulations:**
- **maximum speed** for cars:
100km/h on motorways
80km/h outside town centres
50km/h in town centres
- **give way**: all traffic from the right has the right of way.

5 .6 The petrol station

● **Ordinary, super and lead-free petrol** are all available in Greece, as is diesel. DERV is only permitted in taxis

How many kilometres to the next petrol station, please?	Πόσα χιλιόμετρα είναι ως το πλησιέστερο βενζινάδικο; *pósa hilyómetra íne os to plisiéstero venzinádhiko?*
I would like...litres of..., please	Βάλτε μου... λίτρα *váltemoo...lítra*
– super	Βάλτε μου... λίτρα σούπερ *váltemoo...lítra sóoper*
– leaded	Βάλτε μου... λίτρα απλή βενζίνη *váltemoo...lítra aplí venzíni*
– unleaded	Βάλτε μου... λίτρα αμόλυβδη *váltemoo...lítra amólivdhi*
– diesel	Βάλτε μου... λίτρα ντήζελ *váltemoo...lítra dízel*
I would like...drachmas' worth of petrol, please.	Θα ήθελα υγραέριο για... δραχμές *tha íthela ighraéryo ya...dhrachmés*
Fill her up, please	Γεμίστε το, παρακαλώ *yemísteto, parakaló*
Could you check...?	Ελέγξτε το... , παρακαλώ *eléngxte to ... parakaló*
– the oil level	Ελέγξτε το λάδι, παρακαλώ *eléngxte to ládhi, parakaló*
– the tyre pressure	Ελέγξτε τα λάστιχα, παρακαλώ *eléngxte ta lásticha, parakaló*
Could you change the oil, please?	Μπορείτε να αλλάξετε τα λάδια; *boríte na aláxete ta ládhya?*
Could you clean the windows/the windscreen, please?	Μπορείτε να καθαρίσετε τα τζάμια/το παρμπρίζ; *boríte na katharísete ta tzámya/to parbríz?*
Could you give the car a wash, please?	Μπορείτε να πλύνετε το αυτοκίνητο; *boríte na plínete to aftokínito?*

5 .7 Breakdown and repairs

I'm having car trouble Could you give me a hand?	'Επαθα βλάβη. Μπορείτε να με βοηθήσετε; *épatha vlávi. boríte na me voithísete?*
I've run out of petrol	'Εμεινα από βενζίνη *émina apó venzíni*
I've locked the keys in the car	'Εχω αφήσει τα κλειδιά στο αυτοκίνητο *écho afísi ta klidhyá sto aftokínito*

The car/motorbike/ moped won't start	Το αυτοκίνητο/η μοτοσικλέτα/το μηχανάκι δεν παίρνει μπρος
	to aftokínito/i motosikléta/to michanáki dhembérni bros
Could you contact the ____ recovery service for me, please?	Μπορείτε να τηλεφωνήσετε στην ΕΛΠΑ;
	boríte na tilefonísete tin elpá;
Could you call a garage ____ for me, please?	Μπορείτε να τηλεφωνήσετε σ' ένα γκαράζ;
	boríte na tilefonísete séna garáz?
Could you give me ____ a lift to...?	Μπορείτε να με πάρετε μαζί σας;
	boríte na me párete mazísas?
– a garage/into town? ____	Μπορείτε να με πάτε σ' ένα γκαράζ/στην πόλη;
	boríte na me páte séna garáz/stim bóli?
– a phone booth? ____	Μπορείτε να με πάτε σ' ένα τηλεφωνικό θάλαμο;
	boríte na me páte séna tilefonikó thálamo?
Can we take my ____ bicycle/moped?	Μπορούμε να πάρουμε και το ποδήλατό μου/το μηχανάκι μου;
	boróome na pároome kye to podhílatómoo/to michanákimoo
Could you tow me to ____ a garage?	Μπορείτε να με τραβήξετε σ' ένα γκαράζ;
	boríte na me travíxete séna garáz?
There's probably ____ something wrong with...(See pages 49 and 53)	Πιθανόν να έχει κάτι το...
	pithanón na éhi káti to...
Can you fix it? ____	Μπορείτε να το φτιάξετε;
	boríte na to ftyáxete?
Could you fix my tyre? ____	Μπορείτε να κολλήσετε το λάστιχό μου;
	boríte na kolísete to lastichómoo?
Could you change this ____ wheel?	Μπορείτε ν' αλλάξετε αυτή τη ρόδα;
	boríte naláxete aftí ti ródha?
Can you fix it so it'll ____ get me to...?	Μπορείτε να το φτιάξετε για να μπορώ να πάω μέχρι... ;
	boríte na to ftyáxete ya na boró na páo méchri...?
Which garage can ____ help me?	Ποιό γκαράζ μπορεί να με βοηθήσει;
	pyo garáz borí na me voithísi?
When will my car/bicycle ____ be ready?	Πότε θα είναι έτοιμο το αυτοκίνητό μου/το ποδήλατό μου;
	póte tha íne étimo to avtokínitómoo/to podhilatómoo?
Can I wait for it here? ____	Μπορώ να περιμένω εδώ;
	boró na periméno edhó?
How much will it cost? ____	Πόσο θα κοστίσει;
	póso tha kostísi?
Could you confirm the ____ details of the bill?	Μπορείτε να διευκρινήσετε το λογαριασμό;
	boríte na dhiefkrinísete to loghariazmó?
Can I have a receipt for ____ the insurance?	Μπορείτε να μου δώσετε μια απόδειξη για την ασφάλεια;
	boríte na moo dhósete mya apódhixi ya tin asfálya?

The parts of a bicycle
(the diagram shows the numbered parts)

1	rear lamp	το πίσω φως	*to píso fos*
2	rear wheel	η πισινή ρόδα	*i pisiní ródha*
3	(luggage) carrier	η σχάρα	*i schára*
4	bicycle fork	η κεφαλή διχαλωτού άξονος	*i kefalí dhichalotóo áxonos*
5	bell	το κουδούνι	*to koodhóoni*
6	crank	η μανιβέλα	*i manivéla*
7	gear change	η αλλαγή ταχυτήτων	*i alayí tahitíton*
	wire	το συρματάκι	*to sirmatáki*
	dynamo	το δυναμό	*to dhinamó*
	bicycle trailer	το ποδήλατο με ρυμουλκούμενο καροτσάκι	*to podhílato me rimoolkóomeno karotsáki*
	frame	ο σκελετός	*o skeletós*
8	dress guard	ο προφυλακτήρας φορεμάτων	*o profilaktíras foremáton*
9	chain guard	η αλυσίδα	*i alisídha*
	chain lock	η αλυσίδα (για το κλείδωμα του ποδηλάτου)	*i alisídha (ya to klídhoma too podhilátoo)*
	milometer	το κοντέρ	*o kontér*
	child's seat	η παιδική σέλα	*i pedhikí séla*
10	headlamp	το φανάρι	*to fanári*
	bulb	η λάμπα	*i lámpa*
11	pedal	το πηδάλι	*to pidháli*
12	pump	η τρόμπα	*i trómba*
13	reflector	ο πίσω αντανακλαστήρας	*o píso andanaklistíras*
14	break pad	το τακάκι	*to takáki*
15	brake cable	το καλώδιο του φρένου	*to kalódhyo too frénoo*
16	ring lock	η κυκλική κλειδαριά	*i kiklikí klidharyá*
17	carrier straps	τα λουριά της σχάρας	*ta looryá tis scháras*
	tachometer	το ταχύμετρο	*to tahímetro*
18	spoke	η ακτίνα της ρόδας	*i aktína tis ródhas*
19	mudguard	το φτερό	*o fteró*
20	handlebar	το τιμόνι	*to timóni*
21	chain wheel	η ρόδα της αλυσίδας	*i ródha tis alisídhas*
22	crank axle	ο άξονας του πηδαλιού	*too pidhalyóo áxonas*
	rim	η ζάντα	*i zánda*
23	valve	η αεροβαλβίδα	*i aerovalvídha*
24	valve tube	το σωληνάκι της αεροβαλβίδας	*to solináki tis aerovalvídhas*
25	gear cable	το καλώδιο επιτάχυνσης	*to kalódhyo epitáchinsis*
26	front fork	η μπροστινή φουρκέτα	*i brostiní foorkéta*
27	front wheel	η μπροστινή ρόδα	*i brostiní ródha*
28	seat	η σέλα	*i séla*

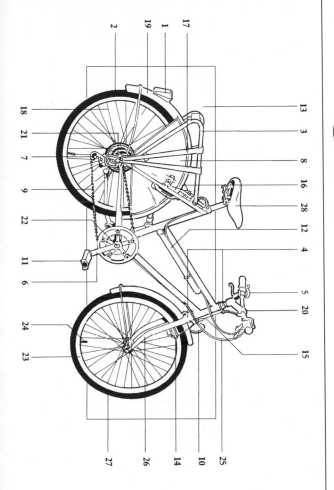

5.8 The bicycle/moped

See the diagram on page 53.

● **Cycle paths** are non-existent in Greece, and little consideration for cyclists is shown on the roads. In tourist places bikes and mopeds can be hired at tourist centres. The maximum speed for mopeds is 40km/h, both inside and outside town centres. Passengers may only be carried on small motorcycles clearly designed with a passenger seat. A crash helmet is advisable.

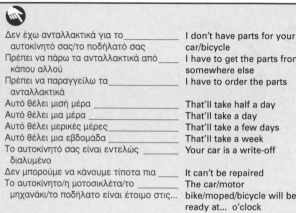

Δεν έχω ανταλλακτικά για το_____ αυτοκίνητό σας/το ποδήλατό σας	I don't have parts for your car/bicycle
Πρέπει να πάρω τα ανταλλακτικά από_____ κάπου αλλού	I have to get the parts from somewhere else
Πρέπει να παραγγείλω τα_____ ανταλλακτικά	I have to order the parts
Αυτό θέλει μισή μέρα _____	That'll take half a day
Αυτό θέλει μια μέρα _____	That'll take a day
Αυτό θέλει μερικές μέρες_____	That'll take a few days
Αυτό θέλει μια εβδομάδα _____	That'll take a week
Το αυτοκίνητό σας είναι εντελώς _____ διαλυμένο	Your car is a write-off
Δεν μπορούμε να κάνουμε τίποτα πια ____	It can't be repaired
Το αυτοκίνητο/η μοτοσικλέτα/το _____ μηχανάκι/το ποδήλατο είναι έτοιμο στις...	The car/motor bike/moped/bicycle will be ready at... o'clock

5.9 Renting a vehicle

I'd like to rent a..._____	Θα ήθελα να νοικιάσω ένα... *tha íthela na nikyáso éna...*
Do I need a (special)_____ licence for that?	Χρειάζομαι μια (ορισμένη) άδεια οδηγήσεως γι' αυτό; *chriázome mya (orizméni) ádhya odhiyíseos yavtó?*
I'd like to rent the...for... ___	Θέλω να νοικιάσω το... για... *thélo na nikyáso to...ya...*
– one day_____	Θέλω να νοικιάσω το... για μία μέρα *thélo na nikyáso to...ya mía méra*
– two days _____	Θέλω να νοικιάσω το... για δύο μέρες *thélo na nikyáso to...ya dhío méres*
How much is that per_____ day/week?	Πόσο κάνει την ημέρα/την εβδομάδα; *póso káni tin iméra/tin evdhomádha?*
How much is the _____ deposit?	Πόσο είναι η εγγύηση; *póso íne i engíisi?*
Could I have a receipt _____ for the deposit?	Μπορείτε να μου δώσετε μια απόδειξη ότι πλήρωσα την εγγύηση; *boríte ne moo dhósete mya apódhixi óti plírosa tin engíisi?*
How much is the _____ surcharge per kilometre?	Πόσο είναι το συμπληρωματικό ποσό για κάθε χιλιόμετρο; *póso íne to simbliromatikó posó ya káthe hilyómetro?*

Does that include petrol?	Είναι αυτό μαζί με τη βενζίνη; *íne aftó mazí me ti venzíni?*
Does that include insurance?	Είναι αυτό μαζί με την ασφάλεια; *íne aftó mazí me tin asfálya?*
What time can I pick the...up tomorrow?	Τι ώρα μπορώ να περάσω αύριο να πάρω το...; *ti óra boró na peráso ávrio na páro to...?*
When does the...have to be back?	Πότε πρέπει να επιστρέψω το... ; *póte prépi na epistrépso to...?*
Where's the petrol tank?	Πού βρίσκεται το ρεζερβουάρ; *poo vrískete to rezervuár?*
What sort of fuel does it take?	Τι είδος καύσιμα χρειάζεται; *ti ídhos káfsima chriázete?*

🔵 .10 Hitchhiking

Where are you heading?	Πού πηγαίνετε; *poo piyénete?*
Can I come along?	Μπορείτε να με πάρετε μαζί σας; *boríte na me párete mazísas?*
Can my boyfriend/ girlfriend come too?	Μπορείτε να πάρετε και το φίλο μου/τη φίλη μου; *boríte na párete kye to fílomoo/ti fílimoo?*
I'm trying to get to...	Εγώ πηγαινω σε... *eghó piyéno se...*
Is that on the way to...?	Βρίσκεται αυτό στο δρόμο για... *vrískete aftó sto dhrómo ya...*
Could you drop me off...?	Μπορείτε να με αφήσετε σε... ; *boríte na me afísete se...?*
– here?	Μπορείτε να με αφήσετε εδώ; *boríte na me afísete edhó?*
– at the exit for...?	Μπορείτε να με αφήσετε στην έξοδο για... ; *boríte na me afísete stin éxodho ya...?*
– in the centre?	Μπορείτε να με αφήσετε στο κέντρο; *boríte na me afísete sto kóndro?*
– at the next roundabout?	Μπορείτε να με αφήσετε στην επόμενη ροτόντα; *boríte na me afísete stin epómeni*
Could you stop here, please?	Μπορείτε να σταματήσετε εδώ, παρακαλώ; *boríte na stamatísete edhó, parakaló?*
I'd like to get out here	Θέλω να κατεβώ εδώ *thélo na katevó edhó*
Thanks for the lift	Ευχαριστώ για την εξυπηρέτηση *efcharistó ya tin exipirétisi*

Public transport

6.1 **I**n general

Announcements

Το τρένο για..., που φεύγει στις...έχει____ καθυστέρηση...λεπτών	The...train to...has been delayed by...minutes
Στη γραμμή...φτάνει τώρα το _____ τρένο για.../από...	The train now arriving at platform...is the...train to.../from...
Στη γραμμή...βρίσκεται ακόμα το _____ τρένο για...	The...train for...is still at platform...
Το τρένο για...φεύγει σήμερα από _____ την πλατφόρμα...	Today the...train to...is due to leave from platform...
Φτάνουμε τώρα στο σταθμό... _____	We're now approaching...

Where does this train____ go to?	Ιού πηγαίνει αυτό το τρένο; *poo piyéni aftó to tréno?*
Does this boat go to...? ____	Αυτό το πλοίο πηγαίνει σε...; *aftó to plío piyéni se ...?*
Can I take this bus to...? ___	Μπορώ να πάω σε...με το λεωφορείο; *boró na páo se ... me to leoforío?*
Does this train stop at...? __	Αυτό το τρένο σταματάει σε...; *aftó to tréno stamatái se ...?*
Is this seat taken/free/ _____ reserved?	Αυτή η θέση είναι πιασμένη/ελεύθερη/κλεισμένη; *aftí i thési íne pyazméni/eléftheri/klizméni?*
I've booked... _____	'Εχω κλείσει... *écho klísi ...*
Could you tell me _____ where I have to get off for...?	Μου λέτε πού πρέπει να κατεβώ για...; *moo léte poo prépi na katevó ya...?*
Could you let me_____ know when we get to...?	Μπορείτε να με προειδοποιήσετε όταν θα φτάνουμε κοντά σε...; *boríte na me proidhopiísete ótan tha ftánoome kondá se...?*
Could you stop at the_____ next stop, please?	Μπορείτε να σταματήσετε στην επόμενη στάση, παρακαλώ; *boríte na stamtísete stin epómeni stási, parakaló?*
Where are we now? _____	Πού είμαστε εδώ; *poo ímaste edhó?*
Do I have to get off here? __	Πρέπει να κατεβώ εδώ; *prépi na katevó edhó?*
Have we already _____ passed...?	Περάσαμε κιόλας...; *perásame kyólas...?*
How long have I_____ been asleep?	Πόση ώρα κοιμήθηκα; *pósi óra kimíthika?*
How long does _____ the...stop here?	Πόση ώρα κάνει στάση εδώ το... ; *pósi óra káni stási edhó to...?*

6 .2 Questions to passengers

Ticket types

Πρώτη ή δεύτερη θέση;_____	First or second class?
Απλό εισιτήριο ή με επιστροφή;_____	Single or return?
Καπνίζοντες ή μη καπνίζοντες;_____	Smoking or non-smoking?
Στο παράθυρο ή στο διάδρομο;_____	Window or aisle?
Μπροστά ή πίσω;_____	Front or back?
Απλή θέση ή κουκέτα;_____	Seat or couchette?
Πάνω, στη μέση ή κάτω;_____	Top, middle or bottom?
Τουριστική θέση ή μπιζνεσκλάς_____	Tourist class or business class?
Καμπίνα ή απλή θέση;_____	Cabin or seat?
Για ένα ή δύο άτομα;_____	Single or double?
Με πόσα άτομα ταξιδεύετε;_____	How many are travelling?

6 .3 Tickets

Can I come back on _____ the same ticket?	Είναι με επιστροφή αυτό το εισιτήριο; *íne me epistrofí aftó to isitírio?*
Can I change on_____ this ticket?	Μπορώ να συνεχίσω μ' αυτό το εισιτήριο; *botó na sinechíso maftó to isitírio?*
How long is this ticket _____ valid for?	Για πόσο καιρό ισχύει αυτό το εισιτήριο; *ya póso kyeró ischíi aftó to isitírio?*
Where can I...? _____	Πού μπορώ να... ; *poo boró na...?*
- buy a ticket? _____	Πού μπορώ να αγοράσω εισιτήριο; *poo boró na aghoráso isitírio?*
- make a reservation?_____	Πού μπορώ να κλείσω θέση; *poo boró na klíso thési?*
- book a flight? _____	Πού μπορώ να κλείσω θέση στο αεροπλάνο; *poo boró na klíso thési sto aeropláno?*
Could I have a...to...,_____ please?	Θέλω ένα...για... *thélo éna...ya...*
- a single _____	Θέλω ένα απλό εισιτήριο για... *thélo éna apló isitírio ya...*
- a return _____	Θέλω ένα μετ επιστροφής για... *thélo éna metepistrofís ya...*
first class _____	πρώτη θέση *próti thési*
second class _____	δεύτερη θέση *dhéfteri thési*
tourist class_____	τουριστική θέση *tooristikí thési*
business class _____	μπιζνεσκλάς *biznesklás*
I'd like to book a _____ seat/couchette/cabin	Θέλω να κλείσω θέση/κρεβάτι/καμπίνα *thélo na klíso thési/kreváti/kabína*
I'd like to book a berth in __ the sleeping car	Θέλω να κλείσω θέση στο βαγκον-λί *thélo na klíso thési sto vagonlí*
top/middle/bottom _____	πάνω/στη μέση/κάτω *páno/sti mési/káto*

Destination

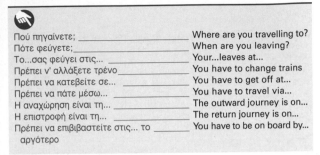

Πού πηγαίνετε; _____	Where are you travelling to?
Πότε φεύγετε; _____	When are you leaving?
Το...σας φεύγει στις... _____	Your...leaves at...
Πρέπει ν' αλλάξετε τρένο _____	You have to change trains
Πρέπει να κατεβείτε σε... _____	You have to get off at...
Πρέπει να πάτε μέσω... _____	You have to travel via...
Η αναχώρηση είναι τη... _____	The outward journey is on...
Η επιστροφή είναι τη... _____	The return journey is on...
Πρέπει να επιβιβαστείτε στις... το _____ αργότερο	You have to be on board by...

Inside the vehicle

Το εισιτήριό σας, παρακαλώ _____	Your ticket, please
Τη βεβαίωση της κράτησης, παρακαλώ ___	Your reservation, please
Το διαβατήριό σας, παρακαλώ _____	Your passport, please
Κάθεστε σε λάθος θέση _____	You're in the wrong seat
Βρίσκεστε σε λάθος... _____	You're on/in the wrong...
Αυτή η θέση είναι κλεισμένη _____	This seat is reserved
Πρέπει να πληρώσετε _____ συμπληρωματικό ποσό	You'll have to pay a supplement
Το... έχει καθυστέρηση... λεπτών_____	The...has been delayed by...minutes

smoking/no smoking _____	καπνίζοντες/μη καπνίζοντες *kapnízondes/mi kapnízondes*
by the window_____	στο παράθυρο *sto paráthiro*
single/double _____	για ένα άτομο/ για δύο άτομα *ya éna átomo/ya dhío átoma*
at the front/back_____	μπροστά/πίσω *brostá/píso*
There are...of us. _____	Είμαστε...άτομα *ímaste...átoma*
with a car_____	Μ' ένα αυτοκίνητο *ména avtokínito*
with a caravan _____	Μ' ένα τροχόσπιτο *ména trochóspito*
with ... bicycles _____	Με .. ποδήλατα *me...podhílata*
Do you also have...? _____	Μήπως έχετε και...; *mípos éhete ke...?*
– season tickets? _____	Μήπως έχετε και κάρτα πολλαπλών διαδρομών; *mípos éhete ke kárta polaplón dhiadhromón?*
– weekly tickets? _____	Μήπως έχετε και κάρτα για μια εβδομάδα; *mípos éhete ke kárta ya mya evdhomáda?*
– monthly tickets? _____	Μήπως έχετε και κάρτα για ένα μήνα; *mípos éhete ke kárta ya éna mína?*

6

Public transport

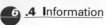

Public transport

Where's...? _____	Πού είναι...;
	poo íne...?
Where's the information ____ desk?	Πού είναι το γραφείο πληροφοριών;
	poo íne to ghrafío pliroforyón?
Where can I find a_____ timetable?	Πού είναι ο πίνακας αφίξεων/αναχωρήσεων;
	poo íne o pínakas afíxeon/anachoríseon?
Where's the...desk? _____	Πού είναι η θυρίδα για...
	poo íne i thirídha ya...?
Do you have a city map_____ with the bus/the underground routes on it?	Μήπως έχετε ένα χάρτη της πόλης με το δίκτυο λεωφορείων/του μετρό;
	mípos éhete éna chárti tis pólis me to díkhtio leoforíon/too metró?
Do you have a _____ timetable?	Μήπως έχετε το ωράριο των δρομολογίων;
	mípos éhete to orário ton dhromoloyíon?
I'd like to confirm/_____ cancel/change my booking for/trip to...	Θέλω να επιβεβαιώσω/ακυρώσω/αλλάξω την κράτησή μου/το ταξίδι μου σε...
	thélo na epiveveóso/akiróso/aláxo tingrátisímoo/to taxídhi moo se...
Will I get my money_____ back?	Θα πάρω πίσω τα λεφτά μου;
	tha páro píso ta leftá moo?
I want to go to... _____ How do I get there?	Πρέπει να πάω σε ... Πώς πάω εκεί το γρηγορότερο;
	prépi na páo se ... Pos páo ekí to ghrighorótero?
How much is a _____ single/return to...?	Πόσο κάνει ένα απλό εισιτήριο/ένα μετ' επιστροφής;
	póso káni éna apló isitírio/éna metepistrofís?
Do I have to pay a_____ supplement?	Πρέπει να πληρώσω συμπληρωματικό εισιτήριο;
	prépi na pliróso simbliromatikó isitírio?
Can I interrupt my_____ journey with this ticket?	Μπορώ να διακόψω το ταξίδι μου μ' αυτό το εισιτήριο;
	boró na dhiakópso to taxídhimoo maftó to isitírio?
How much luggage _____ am I allowed?	Πόσες αποσκευές μπορώ να πάρω μαζί μου;
	póses aposkevés boró na páro mazímoo?
Does this...travel direct? ___	Αυτό το...πηγαίνει κατ' ευθείαν;
	aftó to...piyéni katefthían?
Do I have to change _____ trains/buses/boats? Where?	Πρέπει ν' αλλάξω τρένο/λεωφορείο/πλοίο; Πού;
	prépi naláxo tréno/leoforío/plío? Poo?
Does the plane touch _____ down anywhere en route?	Το αεροπλάνο κάνει ενδιάμεσες προσγειώσεις;
	to aeropláno káni endhiámeses prosyiósis?
Does the boat call in at ____ any ports on the way?	Το πλοίο πιάνει σκάλα και σ' άλλα λιμάνια;
	to plío pyáni skála ke sáala limánya?
Does the train/ _____ bus stop at...?	Το τρένο/το λεωφορείο κάνει στάση σε...;
	to tréno/to leoforío káni stási se...?
Where should I get off? ____	Πού πρέπει να κατεβώ;
	poo prépi na katevó?
Is there a connection _____ to...?	Υπάρχει ανταπόκριση για ...
	ipárchi andapókrisi ya...
How long do I have to ____ wait?	Πόση ώρα πρέπει να περιμένω;
	pósi óra prépi na periméno?
When does...leave?_____	Πότε φεύγει...;
	póte févyi...?

What time does the _____ first/last/next...leave?	Τι ώρα φεύγει το πρώτο/τελευταίο/επόμενο...; *ti óra févyi to próto/teleftéo/epómeno...?*
How long does...take? ____	Πόση ώρα κάνει το...; *pósi óra káni to...?*
What time does...arrive ____ in...?	Τι ώρα φτάνει το...σε...; *ti óra ftáni to...se...?*
Where does the...to... _____ leave from?	Από πού φεύγει το...για...; *apó poo févyi to...ya...?*
Is this...to...? _____	Αυτό είναι το...για...; *aftó íne to...ya...?Δ·ὐ!*

6 .5 Aeroplanes

● **In addition to** scheduled flights from the UK to Athens and Thessaloniki there are a large number of charters to both cities and to Corfu, Kos, Crete and Rhodes. Athens has two airports, one for Olympic Airways and one for other airlines; the two airports are quite close to one another. They have two areas, *αφίξεις* (arrivals) and *αναχωρήσεις* (departures). At the check-in desk you will receive a *δελτίο επιβιβάσεως* (boarding card) and will be told which *έξοδος* (gate) you will be leaving from

In a Greek airport you will find the following signs:

αναχωρήσεις departures	εσωτερικές ανταποκρίσεις	πτήσεις εξωτερικού international flights
αφίξεις arrivals	internal/domestic connecting flights	πτήσεις εσωτερικού domestic flights

6 .6 Trains

● **The rail network** in Greece is not very extensive, but rail travel is generally much cheaper than in the UK. The Greek State Railways company is responsible for the line from Thessaloniki to Athens. Much of the route is single track, and there are innumerable small stations. Another company runs the loop of track from Athens around the Peloponnese. You can travel first or second class, and students, children and groups of more than ten persons can obtain reductions. It is advisable to book a seat at the time you purchase your ticket.

6 .7 Taxis

● **There are plenty** of taxis in Greece and they are usually much cheaper than in the UK. In Athens and Thessaloniki taxis act rather like buses; they pick up and drop off passengers as much as possible. Virtually all taxis have a meter, but it is often possible to agree a price for a longer journey in advance. A supplement is usual for luggage, a journey at night, on a Sunday or bank holiday, or to an airport.

Taxi! _____	ταξί *taxí!*
Could you get me a taxi,___ please?	Μπορείτε να καλέσετε ένα ταξί για μένα; *boríte na kalésete éna taxí ya ména?*
Where can I find a taxi____ around here?	Πού μπορώ να βρω ένα ταξί εδώ κοντά; *poo boró na vro éna taxí edhó kondá?*

ελεύθερο free	κατειλημμένο taken	σταθμός ταξί taxi rank

Could you take me to..., _____ please?
Με πηγαίνετε σε..., παρακαλώ;
me piyénete se..., parakaló?

– this address _____
Με πηγαίνετε σ' αυτή τη διεύθυνση, παρακαλώ;
me piyénete saftí ti dhiéfthinsi, parakaló?

– the...hotel _____
Με πηγαίνετε στο ξενοδοχείο..., παρακαλώ;
me piyénete sto xenodhohío..., parakaló?

– the town/city centre_____
Με πηγαίνετε στο κέντρο, παρακαλώ;
me piyénete sto kéndro, parakaló?

– the station _____
Με πηγαίνετε στο σταθμό, παρακαλώ;
me piyénete sto stathmó, parakaló?

– the airport _____
Με πηγαίνετε στο αεροδρόμιο, παρακαλώ;
me piyénete sto aerodhrómio, parakaló?

How much is the _____ trip to...?
Πόσο κάνει η διαδρομή μέχρι...;
póso káni i dhiadromí méchri...?

How far is it to...? _____
Πόσο μακριά είναι μέχρι... ;
póso makriá íne méchri...?

Could you turn on the _____ meter, please?
Μπορείτε να βάλετε το μετρητή, παρακαλώ;
boríte na válete to metrití, parakaló?

I'm in a hurry _____
Βιάζομαι
vyázome

Could you speed up/slow __ down a little?
Μπορείτε να πηγαίνετε πιο γρήγορα/πιο αργά, παρακαλώ;
boríte na piyénete pyo ghríghora/pyo arghá, parakaló?

Could you take a _____ different route?
Μπορείτε να πάρετε ένα άλλο δρόμο;
boríte na párete éna álo dhrómo?

I'd like to get out here,_____ please
Αφήστε με να κατεβώ εδώ, παρακαλώ
afíste me na katevó edhó, parakaló

You have to go...here _____
Εδώ πρέπει να πάτε...
edhó prépi na páte...

You have to go straight _____ on here
Εδώ πρέπει να πάτε ίσια
edhó prépi na páte ísya

You have to turn left_____ here
Εδώ πρέπει να πάτε αριστερά
edhó prépi na páte aristerá

You have to turn right _____ here
Εδώ πρέπει να πάτε δεξιά
edhó prépi na páte dhexyá

This is it _____
Εδώ είναι
edhó íne

Could you wait a minute___ for me, please?
Μπορείτε να με περιμένετε ένα λεπτό;
boríte na me periménete éna leptó?

Overnight accommodation

Overnight accommodation

7.1 General

● **Hotel accommodation:** hotels (ξενοδοχεία) are in different categories: luxury class, A class, B class, C class, D class, and E class. The classification is somewhat arbitrary, and it is always worth trying a cheap hotel. An expensive hotel will not necessarily be more pleasant or comfortable than a cheaper one.
Most hotels serve breakfast.

Rooms in private houses or pensions are available and offer a cheap and interesting form of accommodation. This is the best way to get to know Greeks. The tourist police can supply you with a list of rooms available in a particular place.

Motels are rare in Greece; they are only to be found close to the motorways.

Youth Hostels exist in the cities; they are divided into male and female sections.

Camping sites are regulated by the Greek National Tourist office (EOT). They are divided into three price levels. There are many sites along the coasts, but they are rarer inland. It is not legal to camp outside such sites.

Πόσο καιρό θέλετε να μείνετε; _____	How long will you be staying?
Μπορείτε να συμπληρώσετε αυτό _____ το έντυπο, παρακαλώ	Fill out this form, please
Το διαβατήριό σας, παρακαλώ _____	Could I see your passport?
Πρέπει να πληρώσετε εγγύηση _____	I'll need a deposit
Πρέπει να προπληρώσετε _____	You'll have to pay in advance

My name's...I've made _____ a reservation over the phone/by mail	Το όνομά μου είναι...'Εκλεισα (τηλεφωνικώς/γραπτά) μια θέση *to onomámoo íne ... éklisa (tilefonikós/ghraptá) mya thési*
How much is it per _____ night/week/ month?	Πόσο κάνει τη νύχτα/την εβδομάδα/το μήνα; *póso káni ti níchta/tin evdhomádha/to mína?*
We'll be staying at _____ least...nights/weeks	Θα μείνουμε τουλάχιστον...νύχτες/εβδομάδες *tha mínoome tooláchiston...níchtes/evdhomádhes*
We don't know yet _____	Δεν ξέρουμε ακόμα ακριβώς *dhen xéroome akóma akrivós*
Do you allow pets _____ (cats/dogs)?	Επιτρέπονται τα κατοικίδια ζώα; *epitréponde ta katikídhia zóa?*
What time does the _____ gate/door open/close?	Τι ώρα κλείνει/ανοίγει η εξώπορτα/η πόρτα; *ti óra klíni/aníyi i exóporta/i pórta?*
Could you get me a taxi, _____ please?	Μου φωνάζετε ένα ταξί, παρακαλώ; *moo fonázete éna taxí, parakaló?*
Where's the manager? _____	Πού είναι ο διαχειριστής; *poo íne o dhiahiristís?*

.2 Camping

See the diagram on page 67.

Διαλέξετε μόνος σας το μέρος _____	You can pick your own site
Εμείς θα σας δείξουμε ένα μέρος _____	You'll be allocated a site
Αυτός είναι ο αριθμός του μέρους σας ___	This is your site number
Να κολλήσετε αυτό στο _____ αυτοκίνητό σας	Stick this on your car, please
Να μην χάσετε αυτή την κάρτα _____	Please don't lose this card

Are we allowed to _____ camp here?	Μπορούμε να κατασκηνώσουμε εδώ; *boróome na kataskinósoome edhó?*
There are...of us and _____ ...tents	Είμαστε...άτομα και...σκηνές *ímaste...átoma ke...skinés*
Can we pick our _____ own site?	Μπορούμε να διαλέξουμε μόνοι μας ένα μέρος; *boróome na dhialéxoome mónimas éna méros?*
Do you have a quiet _____ spot for us?	Έχετε ένα ήσυχο μέρος για μας; *éhete éna ísicho méros ya mas?*
Do you have any other ____ sites available?	Δεν έχετε ένα άλλο μέρος ελεύθερο; *dhen éhete éna álo méros eléfthero?*
It's too windy/sunny/ _____ shady here	Έχει πολύ αέρα/ήλιο/ίσκιο εδώ *éhi polí aéra/ílyo/ískyo edhó*
It's too crowded here _____	Έχει πολλή κίνηση εδώ *éhi polí kínisi edhó*
The ground's too _____ hard/uneven	Το εδαφος είναι πολύ σκληρό/άνισο *to édhafos íne polí skliró/ániso*
Do you have a level _____ spot for the camper/caravan/folding caravan?	Έχετε ένα ίσιο μέρος για το κάμπερ μας/το τροχόσπιτο μας. το λυόμενο τροχόσπιτό μας; *éhete éna ísyo méros ya to kámpermas/to trochóspitómas /to liómeno trochóspitómas*
Could we have adjoining __ pitches?	Μπορούμε να κατασκηνώσουμε δίπλα-δίπλα; *boróome na kataskinósoome dhípla-dhípla?*
Can we park the car _____ next to the tent?	Μπορώ να παρκάρω το αυτοκίνητο δίπλα στη σκηνή; *boró na parkáro to aftokínito dhípla sti skiní?*
How much is it per _____ person/tent/caravan/car?	Πόσο κάνει το άτομο/για μία σκηνή/για ένα τροχόσπιτο/για ένα αυτοκίνητο; *póso káni to átomo/ya mía skiní/ya éna trochóspito/ya éna aftokínito?*
Are there any chalets to ___ rent?	Νοικιάζονται καλύβες; *nikyázonde kalíves?*
Are there any...? _____	Υπάρχουν εδώ...; *ipárchoon edhó...?*
– any hot showers? _____	Υπάρχουν εδώ ντους με ζεστό νερό *ipárchoon edhó doos me zestó neró*
– washing machines? _____	Υπάρχουν εδώ πλυντήρια; *ipárchoon edhó plindíria?*
Is there a...on the site? ____	Υπάρχει σ' αυτό το χώρο...; *ipárchi saftó to chóro...?*
Is there a children's _____ play area on the site?	Υπάρχει σ' αυτό το χώρο μια παιδική χαρά; *ipárchi saftó to chóro mya pedhikí chará?*

Overnight accommodation

Camping equipment
(the diagram shows the numbered parts)

	luggage space	ο χώρος αποσκευών	o chóros aposkevón /
	can opener	το ανοιχτήρι	to anichtíri
	butane gas bottle	η μποτίλια υγραερίου	i botílya ighraeríoo
1	pannier	η τσάντα του ποδηλάτου	i tsánda too podilátoo
2	gas cooker	η κουζίνα υγραερίου	i koozína ighraeríoo
3	groundsheet	το πάτωμα της σκηνής	to pátoma tis skinís
	mallet	το σφυρί	to sfirí
	hammock	η μπράντα	i bránda
4	jerry can	το μπιντόνι	to bidóni
	campfire	η πυρά	i pirá
5	folding chair	η πτυσσόμενη καρέκλα	i ptisómeni karékla
6	insulated picnic box	η τσάντα-ψυγείο	i tsánda-psiyío
	ice pack	ο ψυκτήρας	o psiktíras
	compass	η πυξίδα	i pixídha
	wick	το φυτίλι	to fitíli
	corkscrew	το τιρμπουσόν	to tirboosón
7	airbed	το αερόστρωμα	to aeróstroma
8	airbed plug	το βούλωμα του αεροστρώματος	to vóoloma too aeróstromatos
	pump	το ποδοκίνητο φυσερό	to podhokinitó fiseró
9	awning	το προστέγασμα της σκηνής	to prostéghazma tis skinís
10	karimat	το χαλάκι	to chaláki
11	pan	η κατσαρόλα	i katsaróla
12	pan handle	το χερούλι	to heróoli
	primus stove	η γκαζιέρα	i gazyéra
	zip	το φερμουάρ	to fermwár
13	backpack	το σακίδιο	to sakídhyo
14	guy rope	το σχοινί της σκηνής	to schiní tis skinís
	sleeping bag	ο υπνόσακος	o ipnósekos
15	storm lantern	η λάμπα θύελλας	i lámpa thíelas
	camp bed	το ράντζο	to rántso
	table	το τραπέζι	to trapézi
16	tent	η σκηνή	i skiní
17	tent peg	το πασαλάκι της σκηνής	to pasaláki tis skinís
18	tent pole	ο ορθοστάτης της σκηνής	o orthostátis tis skinís
	vacuum flask	το θερμός	to thermós
19	water bottle	το παγούρι	to paghóori
	clothes peg	το μανταλάκι	to mandaláki
	clothes line	το σχοινί της μπουγάδας	to schiní tis booghádhas
	windbreak	ο ανεμοφράκτης	o anemofráktis
20	torch	ο φακός	o fakós
	pocket knife	ο σουγιάς	o sooyás

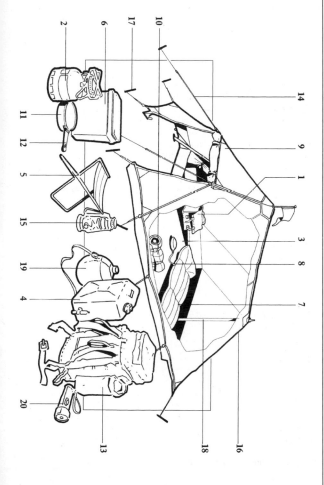

Are there covered _____ cooking facilities on the site?	Υπάρχει σκεπαστός χώρος για μαγείρευμα; *ipárchi skepastós chóros ya mayírevma?*
Can I rent a safe here? _____	Μπορώ να νοικιάσω ένα χρηματοκιβώτιο; *boró na nikyáso éna chrimatokivótyo?*
Are we allowed to_____ barbecue here?	Επιτρέπεται εδώ το μπάρμπεκιου; *epitrépete edhó to barbekyóo?*
Are there any power_____ points?	Υπάρχουν ηλεκτρικές συνδέσεις; *ipárchoon ilektrikés sindhésis?*
Is there drinking water?____	Υπάρχει πόσιμο νερό; *ipárchi pósimo neró?*
When's the rubbish_____ collected?	Πότε μαζεύουν τα σκουπίδια; *póte mazévoon ta skoopídhya?*
Do you sell gas bottles _____ (butane gas/propane gas)?	Πουλάτε φιάλες υγραερίου (πετρογκάζ); *pooláte fyáles ighraeríoo (petrogáz)?*

🄼 .3 Hotel/B&B/apartment/holiday house

Do you have a _____ single/double room available?	Έχετε ένα ελεύθερο μονό/διπλό δωμάτιο; *éhete éna eléfthero monó/dhipló dhomátyo?*
per person/per room _____	το άτομο/το δωμάτιο *to átomo/to dhomátyo*
Does that include _____ breakfast/lunch/dinner?	Με το πρωινό/το μεσημεριανό/το βραδινό; *me to proinó/to mesimeryanó/to vradhinó?*
Could we have two_____ adjoining rooms?	Μπορούμε να έχουμε δύο δωμάτια δίπλα-δίπλα; *boróome na échoome dhío dhomátya dhípla-dhípla?*
with/without _____ toilet/bath/shower	με/χωρίς τουαλέτα/μπάνιο/ντους *me/chorís twaléta/bányo/doos*
(not) facing the street_____	(όχι) από την μεριά του δρόμου *(óhi) apó ti meryá too dhrómoo*
with/without a view _____ of the sea	με/χωρίς θέα προς τη θάλασσα *me/chorís théa pros ti thálasa*
Is there...in the hotel?_____	Το ξενοδοχείο έχει...; *to xenodhohío éhi...?*
Is there a lift in the hotel? __	Το ξενοδοχείο έχει ασανσέρ; *to xenodhohío éhi asansér?*
Do you have _____ room service?	Το ξενοδοχείο έχει εξυπηρέτηση δωματίου/ρουμ σέρβις; *to xenodhohío éhi exipirétisi dhomatíoo/room sérvis*
Could I see the room? _____	Μπορώ να δω το δωμάτιο; *boró na dho to dhomátyo?*
I'll take this room_____	Θα πάρω αυτό το δωμάτιο *tha páro aftó to dhomátyo*
We don't like this one _____	Αυτό το δωμάτιο δε μας αρέσει *aftó to dhomátyo dhe mas arési*
Do you have a larger/_____ less expensive room?	Έχετε ένα μεγαλύτερο/πιο φτηνό δωμάτιο; *éhete éna meghalítero/pyo ftinó dhomátyo?*
Could you put in a cot? ____	Μπορείτε να βάλετε κι ένα παιδικό κρεβάτι στο δωμάτιό μας; *boríte na válete kyéna pedhikó kreváti sto dhomátiómas?*
What time's breakfast? ____	Τί ώρα είναι το πρωινό; *ti óra íne to proinó?*

Where's the dining room?	Πού είναι η τραπεζαρία; *poo íne i trapezaría?*
Can I have breakfast in my room?	Μπορώ να έχω το πρωινό στο δωμάτιό μου; *boró na écho to proinó sto dhomátiomoo?*
Where's the emergency exit/fire escape?	Πού είναι η έξοδος κινδύνου ή η σκάλα πυρκαγιάς; *poo íne i éxodhos kindhínoo/i skála pirkayás?*

Η τουαλέτα και το ντους είναι _____ στον ίδιο όροφο/στο δωμάτιό σας	You can find the toilet and shower on the same floor/en suite
Από δω, παρακαλώ _____	This way, please
Το δωμάτιό σας είναι στο...όροφο, _____ ο αριθμός είναι...	Your room is on the...floor, number...

Where can I park my car (safely)?	Υπάρχει ένα (ασφαλές) μέρος όπου μπορώ να παρκάρω το αυτοκίνητό μου; *ipárchi éna (asfalés) méros ópoo boró na parkáro to aftokínitómoo?*
The key to room..., please	Το κλειδί του δωματίου..., παρακαλώ *to klidhí too dhomatíoo..., parakaló*
Could you put this in the safe, please?	Μπορώ να αφήσω αυτό στο χρηματοκιβώτιό σας; *boró nafíso aftó sto chrimatokivótiósas?*
Could you wake me at...tomorrow?	Μπορείτε να με ξυπνήσετε αύριο στις...; *boríte na me xipnísete ávrio stis ?*
Could you find a babysitter for me?	Μπορείτε να μου βρείτε μια μπέιμπυ σίτερ; *boríte na moo vríte mya béibi-síter?*
Could I have an extra blanket?	Μπορώ να έχω κι άλλη μια κουβέρτα; *boró na écho kyáli mía koovérta?*
What days do the cleaners come in?	Ποιές μέρες καθαρίζουν τα δωμάτια; *pyes méres katharízoon ta dhomátya?*
When are the sheets/towels/tea towels changed?	Πότε αλλάζουν τα σεντόνια/τις πετσέτες/τις πετσέτες για τα πιάτα; *póte alázoon ta sendónya/tis petsétes/tis petsétes ya ta pyáta?*

7.4 Complaints

We can't sleep for the noise	Δεν μπορούμε να κοιμηθούμε μ' αυτό το θόρυβο *dhemboróome na kimithóome maftó to thórivo*
Could you turn the radio down, please?	Μπορείτε να χαμηλώσετε λίγο το ραδιόφωνο; *boríte na chamilósete lígho to radhiófono?*
We're out of toilet paper	Τελείωσε το χαρτί υγείας *telíose to chartí iyías*
There aren't any.../there's not enough...	Δεν έχει/δεν έχει αρκετά... *dhen éhi/dhen éhi arketá...*
The bed linen's dirty	Τα κλινοσκεπάσματα είναι βρώμικα *ta klinoskepázmata íne vromiká*
The room hasn't been cleaned	Δεν καθάρισαν το δωμάτιο *dhen kathárisan to dhomátyo*

The kitchen is not clean____	Η κουζίνα δεν είναι καθαρή
	i koozína dhen íne katharí
The kitchen utensils are____ dirty	Τα κουζινικά είναι βρώμικα
	ta koozjniká íne vrómika
The heater's not____ working	Το καλοριφέρ δε λειτουργεί
	to kalorifér dhe litooryí
There's no (hot) ____ water/electricity	Δεν έχει (ζεστό) νερό/ρεύμα
	dhen éhi (zestó) neró/révma
...is broken____	...χάλασε
	...chálase
Could you have that ____ seen to?	Μπορείτε να το διορθώσετε;
	boríte na to dhiorthósete?
Could I have another ____ room?	Μπορείτε να μου δώσετε ένα άλλο δωμάτιο
	boríte na moo dhósete éna álo dhomátyo
The bed creaks terribly ____	Το κρεβάτι τρίζει φοβερά
	to kreváti trízi foverá
The bed sags terribly ____	Το κρεβάτι βουλιάζει φοβερά
	to kreváti voolyázi foverá
There's a lot of noise ____	Έχει πάρα πολύ θόρυβο
	éhi pára polí thórivo
There are bugs/insects____ in our room	Έχουμε πολλά ζωύφια/έντομα
	échoome polá zoífya/éndoma
This place is full____ of mosquitos	Είναι γεμάτο κουνούπια εδώ
	íne yemáto koonóopya edhó
– cockroaches____	Είναι γεμάτο κατσαρίδες εδώ
	íne yemáto katsarídhes edhó

7.5 Departure

See also 8.2 Settling the bill

I'm leaving tomorrow. ____ Could I settle my bill, please?	Αύριο φεύγω. Μπορώ να πληρώσω τώρα;
	ávrio févgho. boró na pliróso tóra?
What time should we____ vacate?	Τί ώρα πρέπει να φύγουμε από...;
	ti óra prépi na fíghoome apó...?
Could I have my deposit/ __ passport back, please?	Μου δίνετε πίσω την εγγύηση/το διαβατήριό μου;
	moo dhínete píso tin engíisi/to dhiavatíriómoo?
We're in a terrible hurry ___	Βιαζόμαστε πολύ
	vyazómaste polí
Could you forward ____ my mail to this address?	Μπορείτε να στείλετε τα γράμματά μου σ' αυτή τη διεύθυνση;
	boríte na stílete ta ghrámatámoo saftí ti dhiéfthinsi?
Could we leave our____ luggage here until we leave?	Μπορούμε να αφήσουμε τις βαλίτσες μας εδώ μέχρι να φύγουμε;
	boróome nafísoome tis valítses mas edhó méchri na fíghoome?
Thanks for your ____ hospitality	Ευχαριστώ για τη φιλοξενία σας
	efcharistó ya ti filoxeníasas

Money matters

Money matters

● **In general,** banks are open to the public between 8am and 2pm; they are closed on Saturdays. Exchange bureaux are open until 10pm. Money and travellers cheques can also be changed in most of the larger hotels. In the islands the post-offices often have currency changing facilities. To exchange currency a proof of identity is usually required. The sign *ΣΥΝΑΛΛΑΓΜΑ* indicates that money can be exchanged.

.1 Banks

Where can I find a_____ bank/an exchange office around here?	Υπάρχει εδώ κοντά καμιά τράπεζα/κανένα γραφείο συναλλάγματος; *ipárchi edhó kondá kamyá trápeza/kanéna ghrafío sinalághmatos?*
Where can I cash this_____ traveller's cheque/giro cheque?	Πού μπορώ να εξαργυρώσω αυτή την ταξιδιωτική επιταγή/ταχυδρομική επιταγή; *poo boró na exaryiróso aftí tin taxidhiotikí epitayí/ tachidhromikí epitayí?*
Can I cash this...here? _____	Μπορώ εδώ να εξαργυρώσω αυτό το...; *boró edhó na exaryiróso aftó to...?*
Can I withdraw money_____ on my credit card here?	Μπορώ να πάρω λεφτά εδώ με μια πιστωτική κάρτα; *boró na páro leftá edhó me mya pistotikí kárta?*
What's the minimum/_____ maximum amount?	Ποιό είναι το ελάχιστο ποσό/το ανώτατο ποσό; *pyo íne to eláchisto posó/to anótato posó?*
Can I take out less_____ than that?	Μπορώ να πάρω και μικρότερο ποσό; *boró na páro ke mikrótero posó?*
I've had some money_____ transferred here. Has it arrived yet?	Έκανα ένα τηλεγραφικό έμβασμα. Έφτασε το έμβασμα; *ékana éna tileghrafikó émvazma. éftase to émvazma?*
These are the details _____ of my bank in the UK	Αυτά είναι τα στοιχεία της τράπεζάς μου στο Ηνωμένο Βασίλειο *aftá íne ta stihía tis trápezásmoo sto Inoméno Vasílio*
This is my bank/giro_____ number	Αυτός είναι ο αριθμός λογαριασμού μου *aftós íne o arithmós loghariazmóomoo*
I'd like to change _____ some money	Θα ήθελα ν' αλλάξω χρήματα *tha íthela naláxo chrímata*
– pounds into... _____	λίρες στερλίνες για... *líres sterlínes ya...*
– dollars into... _____	δολλάρια για... *dholária ya...*
What's the exchange _____ rate?	Ποιά είναι η ισοτιμία; *pya íne i isotimía?*
Could you give me _____ some small change with it?	Μπορείτε να μου δώσετε και λίγα ψιλά, παρακαλώ; *boríte na moo dhósete ke lígha psilá, parakaló;*
This is not right _____	Αυτό είναι λάθος *avtó íne láthos*

Υπογράψετε εδώ_____	Sign here, please.
Συμπληρώσετε αυτό το χαρτί_____	Fill this out, please.
Μπορώ να δω το διαβατήριό σας; _____	Could I see your passport, please?
Μπορώ να δω την ταυτότητα σας; _____	Could I see some identification, please?
Μπορώ να δω την ταχυδρομική _____ σας κάρτα;	Could I see your girobank card, please?
Μπορώ να δω την τραπεζική _____ σας κάρτα;	Could I see your bank card, please?

8 .2 Settling the bill

Could you put it on_____ my bill?	Μπορείτε να το γράψετε στο λογαριασμό μου; *boríte na to ghrápsete sto loghariazmómoo?*
Does this amount _____ include service?	(Στο ποσό αυτό) συμπεριλαμβάνεται η εξυπηρέτηση; *(sto posó aftó) simberilamvánete i exipirétisi?*
Can I pay by...?_____	Μπορώ να πληρώσω με...; *boró na plíroso me...?*
Can I pay by credit card?___	Μπορώ να πληρώσω με πιστωτική κάρτα; *boró na plíroso me pistotikí kárta?*
Can I pay by traveller's ____ cheque?	Μπορώ να πληρώσω με ταξιδιωτική επιταγή; *boró na plíroso me taxidhyotikí epitayí?*
Can I pay with foreign _____ currency?	Μπορώ να πληρώσω με ξένο συνάλλαγμα; *boró na plíroso me xéno sinálaghma?*
You've given me too _____ much/you haven't given me enough change	Μου δώσατε πίσω πάρα πολλά/πολύ λίγα *moo dhósate píso pára polá/polí lígha*

| Δε δεχόμαστε πιστωτικές _____ κάρτες/ταξιδιωτικές επιταγές/ξένο συνάλλαγμα | We don't accept credit cards/traveller's cheques/foreign currency |

Could you check this _____ again, please?	Μπορείτε να το ξαναελέγξετε, παρακαλώ; *boríte na to xanaelénxete, parakaló?*
Could I have a receipt, _____ please?	Μπορώ να έχω μια απόδειξη/το λογαριασμό; *boró na écho mya apódhixi/to loghariazmó?*
I don't have enough _____ money on me	Δεν έχω αρκετά χρήματα επάνω μου *dhen écho arketá chrímata epánomoo*
This is for you _____	ορίστε, αυτό είναι για σας *oríste, aftó íne ya sas*
Keep the change _____	Κρατήστε τα ρέστα *kratíste ta résta*

Post and telephone

Post and telephone

9.1 Post

For giros, see 8 Money matters

● **In large towns** post offices are open from Monday to Friday between 7.30am and 8pm; in many such towns they are also open on Saturdays. In smaller towns the opening times are variable. Greek post-offices can be recognised by the sign ΕΛΤΑ. Giro cards can be used there.

Stamps (*γραμματόσημα*) are also available in kiosks (*περίπτερα*) and in tourist areas they are often also sold in small souvenir and postcard shops.

γραμματόσημα stamps δέματα parcels	ταχυδρομικές επιταγές money orders	τηλεγραφήματα telegrams

Where's...? _____	Πού είναι...; *poo íne...?*
Where's the post office? ___	Υπάρχει εδώ κοντά κανένα ταχυδρομείο; *ipárchi edhó kondá kanéna tahidhromío?*
Where's the main post office? _____	Πού είναι το κεντρικό ταχυδρομείο; *poo íne to kendrikó tahidhromío?*
Where's the postbox? _____	Υπάρχει εδώ κοντά ένα γραμματοκιβώτιο; *ipárchi edhó kondá éna ghramatokivótyo?*
Which counter should I go to...? _____	Σε ποιά θυρίδα πρέπει να πάω για...; *se pya thirídha prépi na páo ya...?*
– to send a fax _____	Σε ποιά θυρίδα πρέπει να πάω για να στείλω ένα φαξ; *se pya thirídha prépi na páo ya na stílo éna fax?*
– to change money _____	Σε ποιά θυρίδα πρέπει να πάω για να αλλάξω χρήματα; *se pya thirídha prépi na páo ya naláxo chrímata?*
– to change giro cheques __	Σε ποιά θυρίδα πρέπει να πάω για να εξαργυρώσω τα ταχυδρομικά τσεκ; *se pya thirídha prépi na páo ya na exaryiróso ta tahidhromiká tsek?*
– for a Telegraph Money Order? __	Σε ποιά θυρίδα πρέπει να πάω για τηλεγραφικό έμβασμα; *se pya thirídha prépi na páo ya tileghrafikó émvazma?*
Poste restante _____	Ποστ-ρεστάντ *post-restánt*
Is there any mail for me? __ My name's...	Έχετε γράμματα για μένα; Το όνομά μου είναι... *éhete ghrámata ya ména? to ónomámoo íne...*

Stamps

What's the postage _____ for a...to...?	Τί γραμματόσημα χρειάζομαι για...; *ti ghramatósima chriázome ya...?*
Are there enough _____ stamps on it?	Φτάνουν αυτά τα γραμματόσημα; *ftánoon aftá ta ghramatósima*
I'd like... ...drachma _____ stamps	Θα ήθελα...γραμματόσημα των... *tha íthela...ghramatósima ton...*
I'd like to send this... _____	Θέλω να το στείλω αυτό ... *thélo na to stílo aftó...*
– express _____	Θέλω να το στείλω αυτό επείγον *thélo na to stílo aftó epíghon*
– by air mail _____	Θέλω να το στείλω αυτό αεροπορικώς *thélo na to stílo aftó aeroporikós*
– by registered mail _____	Θέλω να το στείλω αυτό συστημένο *thélo na to stílo aftó sistiméno*

Telegram / fax

I'd like to send a _____ telegram to...	Θα ήθελα να στείλω ένα τηλεγράφημα σε... *tha íthela na stílo éna tileghráfima se...*
How much is that _____ per word?	Πόσο κάνει η λέξη; *póso káni i léxi?*
This is the text I want _____ to send	Αυτό είναι το κείμενο που θέλω να στείλω *aftó íne to kímeno poo thélo na stílo*
Shall I fill out the form _____ myself?	Να συμπληρώσω μόνος/μόνη μου το έντυπο; *na simpliróso mónos/móni moo to éndipo?*
Can I make photocopies/___ send a fax here?	Μπορώ να κάνω φωτοτυπίες/να στείλω ένα φαξ; *boró edhó na káno fototipíes/na stílo éna fax?*
How much is it _____ per page?	Πόσο κάνει η σελίδα; *póso káni i selídha?*

9.2 Telephone

See also 1.8 Telephone alphabet

● **In Greece** you cannot make phone calls from an ordinary post office. The special telephone offices are marked OTE. Here you make the call and then pay. In tourist resorts there are also usually a number of public phone-boxes (for which a phone-card is advisable) from which you can make international calls, and local calls can be made from kiosks.

When phoning someone in Greece, you will not be greeted with the subscriber's name or number, but simply with *εμπρός* or *ορίστε*.

Is there a phone box _____ around here?	Υπάρχει εδώ κοντά κανένας τηλεφωνικός θάλαμος; *ipárchi edhó kondá kanénas tilefonikós thálamos?*
Could I use your _____ phone, please?	Μπορώ να χρησιμοποιήσω το τηλέφωνό σας; *boró na chrisimopiíso to tiléfonósas?*
Do you have a _____ (city/region)...phone directory?	Εχετε ένα τηλεφωνικό κατάλογο της πόλης.../της περιοχής...; *éhete éna tilefonikó katálogho tis pólis/tis periohís...?*
Could you give me...? _____	Μπορείτε να μου δώσετε...; *boríte na moo dhósete...?*

– the number for international directory enquiries	Μπορείτε να μου δώσετε τον αριθμό για τις πληροφορίες εξωτερικού; *boríte na moo dhósete ton airithmó ya tis pliroforíes exoterikóo?*
– the number of room... ___	Μπορείτε να μου δώσετε τον αριθμό του δωματίου; *boríte na moo dhósete ton arithmó too dhomatíoo...?*
– the international _____ access code	Μπορείτε να μου δώσετε το διεθνή κωδικό της/του/των...; *boríte na moo dhósete to dhiethní kódhiko tis/too/ton...?*
– the country code for...____	Μπορείτε να μου δώσετε τον κωδικό της...; *boríte na moo dhósete tongódhiko tis...?*
– the trunk code for... _____	Μπορείτε να μου δώσετε τον κωδικό της πόλης...; *boríte na moo dhósete tongódhiko tis pólis...?*
– the number of... _____	Μπορείτε να μου δώσετε τον αριθμό τηλεφώνου του/της...; *boríte na moo dhósete ton arithmó tilefónoo too/tis...?*
Could you check if this ____ number's correct?	Μπορείτε να ελέγξετε αν είναι σωστός αυτός ο αριθμός; *boríte na elénxete an íne sostós o arithmós?*
Can I dial international____ direct?	Μπορώ να τηλεφωνήσω αυτόματα στο εξωτερικό; *boró na tilefoníso aftómata sto exoterikó?*
Do I have to go through ___ the switchboard?	Πρέπει να τηλεφωνήσω μέσω της τηλεφωνήτριας; *prépi na tilefoníso méso tis tilefonítrias?*
Do I have to dial '0' first? __	Πρέπει να πάρω πρώτα το μηδέν; *prépi na páro próta to midhén?*
Do I have to book _____ my calls?	Πρέπει να ζητήσω μια συνδιάλεξη; *prépi na zitíso mya sindhiálexi?*
Could you dial this _____ number for me, please?	Μπορείτε να μου πάρετε τον εξής αριθμό, παρακαλώ; *boríte na moo párete ton exís arithmó, parakaló?*
Could you put me _____ through to.../extension..., please?	Μπορείτε να με συνδέσετε με.../με το εσωτερικό τηλέφωνο...; *boríte na me sindhésete me.../me to esoterikó tiléfono...?*
I'd like to place a _____ reverse-charge call to...	Θέλω να τηλεφωνήσω με έξοδα του δέκτη... *thélo na thlefoníso me éxodha too dhékti...*
What's the charge per _____ minute?	Πόσο κάνει το λεπτό; *póso káni to leptó?*
Have there been any _____ calls for me?	Μου τηλεφώνησε κανείς; *moo tilefónise kanís?*

The conversation

Who is this, please? _____	Ποιός είναι; *pyos íne?*
Hello, this is... _____	Γειά σας, είμαι ο/η... *Yásas, íme o/i...*

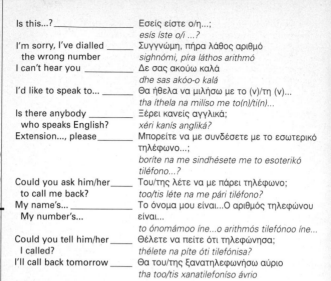

Is this...? _____ Εσείς είστε ο/η...;
esís íste o/i ...?

I'm sorry, I've dialled _____ Συγγνώμη, πήρα λάθος αριθμό
the wrong number *sighnómi, píra láthos arithmó*

I can't hear you _____ Δε σας ακούω καλά
dhe sas akóo-o kalá

I'd like to speak to... _____ Θα ήθελα να μιλήσω με το (ν)/τη (ν)...
tha íthela na milíso me to(n)/ti(n)...

Is there anybody _____ Ξέρει κανείς αγγλικά;
who speaks English? *xéri kanís angliká?*

Extension..., please_____ Μπορείτε να με συνδέσετε με το εσωτερικό
τηλέφωνο...;
*boríte na me sindhésete me to esoterikó
tiléfono...?*

Could you ask him/her_____ Του/της λέτε να με πάρει τηλέφωνο;
to call me back? *too/tis léte na me pári tiléfono?*

My name's... _____ Το όνομα μου είναι...Ο αριθμός τηλεφώνου
My number's... είναι...
to ónomámoo íne...o arithmós tilefónoo íne...

Could you tell him/her _____ Θέλετε να πείτε ότι τηλεφώνησα;
I called? *thélete na píte óti tilefónisa?*

I'll call back tomorrow _____ Θα του/της ξανατηλεφωνήσω αύριο
tha too/tis xanatilefoníso ávrio

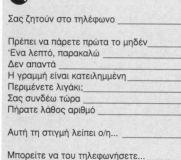

Σας ζητούν στο τηλέφωνο _____ There's a phone call for you

Πρέπει να πάρετε πρώτα το μηδέν_____ You have to dial '0' first

Ένα λεπτό, παρακαλώ _____ One moment, please

Δεν απαντά _____ There's no answer

Η γραμμή είναι κατειλημμένη_____ The line's engaged

Περιμένετε λιγάκι; _____ Do you want to hold?

Σας συνδέω τώρα _____ Putting you through

Πήρατε λάθος αριθμό _____ You've got a wrong number

Αυτή τη στιγμή λείπει ο/η... _____ He's/she's not here right now

Μπορείτε να του τηλεφωνήσετε... _____ He'll/she'll be back...

Αυτός είναι ο αυτόματος τηλεφωνητής του/της... _____ This is the answering machine of...

Shopping

Shopping

● **Opening times:** in general shops are open on Mondays, Wednesdays and Saturdays from 8am until 2.30pm and on Tuesdays, Thursdays and Fridays from 8am to 1pm and from 5pm to 8pm. In tourist areas in the summer, however, most shops open every evening and stay open until late. In the big cities opening hours vary, and many shops remain open throughout the day.

αγορά market	κατάστημα αθλητικών ειδών sports shop	περίπτερο kiosk
ανθοπωλείο florist's	κατάστημα παιχνιδιών toy shop	πλυντήριο laundry
αρτοπωλείο (φούρνος) bakery	κατάστημα σουβενίρ souvenir shop	πολυκατάστημα department store
βιβλιοπωλείο bookshop	κοινόχρηστο πλυντήριο	πρακτορείο ταξιδιών travel agency
γαλακτοπωλείο dairy product shop	laundrette κομμωτήριο	ραφείο tailor's
γουναράδικο furrier's	ladies' hairdresser's κοσμηματοπωλείο	σούπερ-μάρκετ supermarket
ζαχαροπλαστείο confectioner's (also acts as a café for its products)	jeweller's κουρείο barber's shop	στεγνοκαθαριστήριο dry cleaner's τσαγκάρης cobbler's
ινστιτούτο καλλονής beauty salon	κρεοπωλείο butcher's shop	υποδηματοπωλείο (παπουτσάδικο)
ιχθυοπωλείο (ψαράδικο) fishmonger's	μανάβικο greengrocer's μοδίστρια	shoe shop φαρμακείο chemist's
καθαριστήριο cleaner's	dressmaker's οπτικός	φωτογραφείο photographer's/
καπελάδικο hat shop	optician's παλαιοπωλείο	camera shop χαρτοπωλείο
καπνοπωλείο tobacconist's	antique shop παντοπωλείο general store	stationer's ψιλικατζίδικο haberdasher's

.1 Shopping conversations

Where can I get...? _____	Σε ποιό κατάστημα μπορώ να βρω...; *se pyo katástima boró na vro...?*
When does this shop _____ open?	Τι ώρα ανοίγει αυτό το μαγαζί; *ti óra aníyi aftó to maghazí?*
Could you tell me _____ where the...department is?	Μπορείτε να μου πείτε πού είναι το τμήμα...; *boríte na moo píte poo íne to tmíma...?*
Could you help me, _____ please? I'm looking for...	Μπορείτε να με βοηθήσετε; Ψάχνω... *boríte na me voithísete? Psáchno...*
Do you sell English/ _____ American newspapers?	Πουλάτε αγγλικές/αμερικανικές εφημερίδες; *pooláte anglikés/amerikanikés efimerídhes?*

| Σας εξυπηρετεί κανείς; _____ | Are you being served? |

No, I'd like... _____ | 'Οχι. Θα ήθελα...
| *óhi. tha íthela...*
I'm just looking, _____ | Θα ρίξω μια ματιά, αν επιτρέπεται
if that's all right | *tha ríxo mya matyá, an epitrépete*

| Τίποτ' άλλο; _____ | Anything else? |

Yes, I'd also like... _____ | Ναι, θέλω και...
| *ne, thélo ke...*
No, thank you. That's all ___ | 'Οχι, ευχαριστώ. Τίποτ' άλλο
| *óhi, efcharistó. típotálo*
Could you show me...? ____ | Μπορείτε να μου δείξετε...
| *boríte na moo dhíxete*
I'd prefer... _____ | Προτιμώ...
| *protimó...*
This is not what I'm _____ | Δεν είναι αυτό που ψάχνω
looking for | *dhen íne aftó poo psáchno*
Thank you. I'll keep_____ | Ευχαριστώ. Θα κοιτάξω και αλλού
looking | *efcharistó. tha kitáxo ke alóo*
Do you have _____ | Μήπως έχετε κάτι που είναι...
something...? | *mípos éhete káti poo íne...*
– less expensive?_____ | Μήπως έχετε κάτι πιο φτηνό;
| *mípos óhete káti pyo ftinó?*
– something smaller? _____ | Μήπως έχετε κάτι πιο μικρό;
| *mípos éhete káti pyo mikró?*
– something larger? _____ | Μήπως έχετε κάτι πιο μεγάλο;
| *mípos éhete káti pyo meghálo?*
I'll take this one _____ | Θα πάρω αυτό
| *tha páro avtó*
Does it come with _____ | Έχει οδηγίες χρήσεως μέσα;
instructions? | *éhi odhiyíes chríseos mésa?*
It's too expensive _____ | Είναι πολύ ακριβό
| *íne polí akrivó*
I'll give you... _____ | Θα σας δώσω...
| *tha sas dhóso...*
Could you keep this for ____ | Μπορείτε να φυλάξετε αυτό για μένα; Θα
me? I'll come back for it | περάσω σε λίγο να το πάρω
later | *boríte na filáxete aftó ya ména? tha peráso*
| *se lígho na to páro*
Have you got a bag _____ | Μου δίνετε μία σακούλα, παρακαλώ;
for me, please? | *moo dhínete mya sakóola, parakaló?*
Could you giftwrap_____ | Μπορείτε να το τυλίξετε για δώρο,
it, please? | παρακαλώ;
| *boríte na to tilíxete ya dhóro, parakaló?*

Shopping

10

Λυπάμαι, δεν το έχουμε _____	I'm sorry, we don't have that
Λυπάμαι, μας έχει εξαντληθεί _____	I'm sorry, we're sold out
Λυπάμαι, θα το έχουμε πάλι... _____	I'm sorry, that won't be in until...
Μπορείτε να πληρώσετε στο ταμείο _____	You can pay at the cash desk
Δε δεχόμαστε πιστωτικές κάρτες _____	We don't accept credit cards
Δε δεχόμαστε ταξιδιωτικές επιταγές _____	We don't accept traveller's cheques
Δε δεχόμαστε ξένο συνάλλαγμα _____	We don't accept foreign currency

🔟 .2 Food

I'd like a hundred _____ grams of..., please	Θα ήθελα εκατό γραμμάρια ... *ha íthela ekató ghramárya...*
– half a kilo of... _____	Θα ήθελα μισό κιλό... *tha íthela misó kiló...*
– a kilo of... _____	Θα ήθελα ένα κιλό *tha íthela éna kiló...*
Could you...it for me, _____ please?	Μπορείτε να μου το...: *boríte na moo to...*
Could you slice it/ _____ dice it for me, please?	Μπορείτε να μου το κόψετε σε φέτες/σε κομμάτια; *boríte na moo to kópsete se fétes/se komátya?*
Could you grate it _____ for me, please?	Μπορείτε να μου το τρίψετε; *boríte na moo to trípsete?*
Can I order it? _____	Μπορώ να το παραγγείλω; *boró na to paranghílo?*
I'll pick it up tomorrow/ _____ at...	Θα περάσω αύριο/στις...να το πάρω *tha peráso ávrio/stis...na to páro*
Can you eat/drink this? _____	Αυτό τρώγεται/πίνεται; *aftó tróyete/pínete?*
What's in it? _____	Τί έχει μέσα; *ti éhi mésa?*

🔟 .3 Clothing and shoes

I saw something in the _____ window. Shall I point it out?	Είδα κάτι στη βιτρίνα. Να σας το δείξω; *ídha káti sti vitrína. na sas to dhíxo?*
I'd like something to _____ go with this	Θέλω κάτι που να ταιριάζει μ' αυτό *thélo káti poo na teryázi maftó*
Do you have shoes _____ to match this?	Έχετε ασορτί παπούτσια; *éhete asortí papóotsya?*
I'm a size...in the UK _____	Στο Ηνωμένο Βασίλειο φοράω νούμερο... *sto inoméno vasílio foráo nóomero...*
Can I try this on? _____	Μπορώ να το δοκιμάσω; *boró na to dhokimáso?*
Where's the fitting room? _____	Πού είναι το δοκιμαστήριο; *poo íne to dhokimastírio*

It doesn't fit _____	Δε μου κάνει	
	dhe moo káni	
This is the right size _____	Αυτό είναι το σωστό νούμερο	
	aftó íne to sostó nóomero	
It doesn't suit me_____	Δε μου πάει	
	dhe moo pái	
Do you have this/ _____	Το έχετε και σε...;	
these in...?	*to éhete ke se...?*	
The heel's too high/low ____	Το τακούνι είναι πολύ ψηλό/χαμηλό	
	to takóoni íne polí psiló/chamiló	
Is this/are these _____	Είναι αυτό/αυτά από γνήσιο δέρμα;	
genuine leather?	*íne aftó/aftá apó ghnísyo dhérma?*	
I'm looking for a... _____	Ψάχνω ένα...για ένα μωρό/παιδί...χρονών	
for a...-year-old baby/child	*psáchno éna...ya éna moró/pedhí...chronón*	
I'd like a...(made of)..._____	Θα ήθελα ένα...από...	
	tha íthela éna...apó...	
– silk _____	Θα ήθελα ένα...από μετάξι	
	tha íthela éna...apó metáxi	
– cotton _____	Θα ήθελα ένα...από βαμβάκι	
	tha íthela éna...apó vamváki	
– woollen _____	Θα ήθελα ένα...από μαλλί	
	tha íthela éna...apó malí	
– linen _____	Θα ήθελα ένα...από λινό	
	tha íthela éna...apó linó	
What temperature_____	Σε ποιά θερμοκρασία μπορώ να το πλύνω;	
can I wash it at?	*se pya thermokrasía boró na to plíno?*	
Will it shrink in the _____	Δε μαζεύει;	
wash?	*dhe mazévi?*	

Καθαριστήριο	Με το χέρι	Μην το στεγνώνετε
dry clean	by hand	στο στεγνωτήριο
Κρεμάστε το	Μη	do not tumble dry
υγρό	σιδερώνετε	Στο πλυντήριο
do no spin dry	do not iron	machine wash

At the cobbler's

Could you mend _____	Μπορείτε να φτιάξετε αυτά τα παπούτσια;
these shoes?	*boríte na ftyáchete aftá ta papóotsya?*
Could you put new _____	Μπορείτε να βάλετε καινούριες
soles/heels on these?	σόλες/καινούρια τακούνια σ΄ αυτά;
	boríte na válete kenóoryes sóles/kenóorya
	takóonya saftá?
When will they be _____	πότε θα είναι έτοιμα;
ready?	*póte tha íne étima?*
I'd like... _____	Θα ήθελα...
	tha íthela...
– a tin of shoe polish _____	Θα ήθελα ένα κουτάκι βερνίκι
	tha íthela éna kootáki verníki papootsyón
– a pair of shoelaces_____	Θα ήθελα ένα ζευγάρι κορδόνια
	tha íthela éna zevghári kordhónya

I'd like a film for this _____ camera, please	Θα ήθελα ένα φιλμ για αυτή τη μηχανή *ha íthela éna film ya avtí ti mihaní*
– a one twenty-six _____ cartridge	Θα ήθελα μια κασέτα των 126 *tha íthela mya kaséta ton ekató íkosi éxl*
– a slide film _____	Θα ήθελα ένα φιλμ για σλάιτς *tha íthela éna film ya slaidz*
– a film cartridge _____	Θα ήθελα μια κασέτα φιλμ *tha íthela mya kaséta film*
– a videotape _____	Θα ήθελα μια βιντεοταινία *tha íthela mya videotenía*
colour/black and white _____	έγχρωμο/ασπρόμαυρο *énchromo/asprómavro*
super eight _____	σούπερ οχτώ *sóoper ochtó*
12/24/36 exposures _____	δωδεκάρι/εικοσιτεσσάρι/τριανταεξάρι *dhodekári/ikositesári/triandaexári*
ASA/DIN number _____	αριθμό ΑΣΑ *arithmó asa*
daylight film _____	φιλμ για κανονικό φως *film ya kanonikó fos*
film for artificial light _____	φιλμ για τεχνητό φως *film ya technitó fos*

Problems

Could you load the _____ film for me, please?	Μπορείτε να βάλετε το φιλμ στη μηχανή, παρακαλώ; *boríte na válete to film sti michaní, parakaló*
Could you take the film _____ out for me, please?	Μπορείτε να βγάλετε το φιλμ από τη μηχανή, παρακαλώ; *boríte na vghálete to film apó ti michaní, parakaló*
Should I replace _____ the batteries?	Πρέπει ν' αλλάξω τις μπαταρίες; *prépi naláxo tis bataríes?*
Could you have a look _____ at my camera, please? It's not working	Μπορείτε να κοιτάξετε τη μηχανή μου; Δε λειτουργεί *boríte na kitáxete ti michanímoo? dhe litooryí*
The...is broken _____	Το...είναι χαλασμένο *to...íne chalazméno*
The film's jammed _____	Το φιλμ έχει μπλεχτεί *to film éhi blechtí*
The film's broken _____	Το φιλμ κόπηκε *to film kópike*
The flash isn't working _____	Το φλας δε λειτουργεί *to flash dhe litooryí*

Processing and prints

I'd like to have this film _____ developed/printed, please	Θα ήθελα να εμφανίσετε/εκτυπώσετε αυτό το φιλμ *tha íthela na emfanísete/ektipósete aftó to film*
I'd like...prints from _____ each negative	Θα ήθελα...φωτογραφίες από κάθε αρνητικό *tha íthela...fotohrafíes apó káthe arnitikó*
glossy/matt _____	γυαλιστερό/ματ *yalisteró/mat*

Shopping

10

6x9 _____	έξι επί εννιά
	éxi epí enyá
I'd like to reorder _____ these photos	Θέλω να παραγγείλω κι άλλες φωτογραφίες απ' αυτές
	thélo na parangílo kyáles fotoghrafíes apaftés
I'd like to have this _____ photo enlarged	Θα ήθελα να μου μεγεθύνετε αυτή τη φωτογραφία
	tha íthela na moo meyethínete aftí ti fotoghrafía
How much is _____ processing?	Πόσο κάνει η εμφάνιση;
	póso káni i emfánisi?
– printing _____	Πόσο κάνει η εκτύπωση;
	póso káni i ektíposi?
– it to re-order _____	Πόσο κάνει η παραγγελία έξτρα φωτογραφιών;
	póso káni i paranghelía éxtra fotoghrafyón?
– the enlargement _____	Πόσο κάνει η μεγέθυνση;
	póso káni i meyénthisi?
When will they _____ be ready?	Πότε θα είναι έτοιμες;
	póte tha íne étimes?

🔟 .5 At the hairdresser's

Do I have to make an _____ appointment?	Πρέπει να κλείσω ραντεβού;
	prépi na klíso randevóo?
Can I come in straight _____ away?	Μπορείτε να με εξυπηρετήσετε αμέσως;
	boríte na me exipiritísete amésos?
How long will I have _____ to wait?	Πόση ώρα πρέπει να περιμένω;
	pósi óra prépi na periméno?
I'd like a shampoo/ _____ haircut	Θα ήθελα να λούσετε/κόψετε τα μαλλιά μου
	tha íthela na lóosete/kópsete ta malyámoo
I'd like a shampoo for _____ oily/dry hair, please	Θα ήθελα ένα σαμπουάν για λιπαρά/ξηρά μαλλιά
	tha íthela éna sampwán ya lipará/xirá malyá
an anti-dandruff _____ shampoo	Θα ήθελα ένα σαμπουάν κατά της πιτυρίδας;
	tha íthela éna sampwán katá tis pitirídhas
– a shampoo for _____ permed/coloured hair	Θα ήθελα ένα σαμπουάν για μαλλιά με περμανάντ/για βαμμένα μαλλιά
	tha íthela éna sampwán ya malyá me permanánt/ya vaména malyá
– a colour rinse shampoo __	Θα ήθελα ένα σαμπουάν με χρώμα
	tha íthela éna sampwán me chróma
– a shampoo with _____ conditioner	Θα ήθελα ένα σαμπουάν με κρέμα λουσίματος
	tha íthela éna sampwán me kréma loosímatos
– highlights _____	Θα ήθελα ένα κουπ-σολέι
	tha íthela éna koop-soléi
Do you have a colour_____ chart, please?	Έχετε ένα δειγματολόγιο χρωμάτων;
	éhete éna dhighmatolóyio chromáton?
I want to keep it the _____ same colour	Θέλω να κρατήσω το ίδιο χρώμα
	thélo na kratíso to ídhyo chróma
I'd like it darker/lighter _____	Τα θέλω πιο σκούρα/πιο ανοιχτά
	ta thélo pyo skóora/pyo anichtá

I'd like a short fringe _____	Θέλω τη φράντζα μου πιο κοντή
	thélo ti frándza moo pyo kondí
Not too short at the back __	Θέλω να μην είναι πολύ κοντά πίσω
	thélo na min íne polí kondá píso
Not too long here _____	Θέλω να μην είναι πολύ μακριά εδώ
	thélo na min íne polí makriá edhó
I'd like/I don't want _____ (many) curls	(Δε) θέλω να έχω (πολλές) μπούκλες
	(dhe) thélo na écho (polés) bóokles
It needs a little/ _____ a lot taken off	Τα θέλω λίγο πιο κοντά/πολύ πιο κοντά
	ta thélo lígho pyo kondá /polí pyo kondá
I want a completely _____ different style	Θέλω τελείως διαφορετικό στυλ
	thélo telíos dhiaforetikó stil
I'd like it the same... _____	Θέλω τα μαλλιά μου σαν...
	thélo ta malyámoo san...
– as that lady's _____	Θέλω τα μαλλιά μου σαν αυτής της κυρίας
	thélo ta malyámoo san aftís tis kirías
– as in this photo_____	Θέλω τα μαλλιά μου όπως σ' αυτή τη φωτογραφία
	thélo ta malyámoo ópos saftí ti fotoghrafía
Could you put the _____ drier up/down a bit?	Μπορείτε να βάλετε την κάσκα πιο ψηλά/πιο χαμηλά;
	boríte na válete tingáska pyo psilá/pyo chamilá?
I'd like a facial_____	Θα ήθελα μια μάσκα προσώπου
	tha íthela mya máska prosópoo
– a manicure _____	Θα ήθελα ένα μανικιούρ
	tha íthela éna manikyóor
– a massage _____	Θα ήθελα ένα μασάζ
	tha íthela éna masáz
Could you trim my..., _____ please?	Μπορείτε να κόψετε λίγο...μου, παρακαλώ;
	boríte na kópsete lígho...moo, parakaló?
Could you trim_____ my fringe?	Μπορείτε να κόψετε λίγο τη φράντζα μου, παρακαλώ;
	boríte na kópsete lígho ti frándzamoo, parakaló?
– my beard? _____	Μπορείτε να κόψετε λίγο τα γένια μου, παρακαλώ;
	boríte na kópsete lígho ta yényamoo, parakaló?
– my moustache? _____	Μπορείτε να κόψετε λίγο το μουστάκι μου, παρακαλώ;
	boríte na kópsete lígho to moostákimoo, parakaló?
I'd like a shave, please_____	Ξύρισμα, παρακαλώ
	xírizma, parakaló
I'd like a wet shave, _____ please	Θέλω να με ξυρίσετε με ξυράφι, παρακαλώ
	thélo na me xirísete me xiráfi, parakaló

Πώς θέλετε να κόψω τα μαλλιά σας; _____	How do you want it cut?
Πιο στυλ θέλετε; _____	What style did you have in mind?
Τί χρώμα θέλετε; _____	What colour did you want it?
Είναι καλή αυτή η θερμοκρασία; _____	Is the temperature all right for you?
Θέλετε κάτι να διαβάσετε; _____	Would you like something to read?
Θέλετε να πιείτε κάτι; _____	Would you like a drink?
Σας αρέσει έτσι; _____	Is this what you had in mind?

At the Tourist Information Centre

11 At the Tourist Information Centre

11 .1 Places of interest

Where's the Tourist Information Centre, please?
Πού βρίσκεται το γραφείο τουρισμού;
poo vrískete to grhafío toorizmóo?

Do you have a city map?
Έχετε ένα χάρτη της πόλης;
éhete éna chárti tis pólis?

Could you give me some information about...?
Μπορείτε να μου δώσετε πληροφορίες για...
boríte na moo dhósete pliroforíes ya ...

How much is that?
Πόσο σας οφείλουμε;
póso sas ofíloome?

What are the main places of interest?
Ποιά είναι τα σπουδαιότερα αξιοθέατα;
pya íne ta spoodheótera axiothéata?

Could you point them out on the map?
Μπορείτε να τα δείξετε στο χάρτη;
boríte na to dhíxete sto chárti?

What do you recommend?
Τί μας συμβουλεύετε;
ti mas simvoolévete?

We'll be here for a few hours
Θα μείνουμε εδώ λίγες ώρες
tha mínoome edhó líyes óres

– a day
Θα μείνουμε εδώ μία μέρα
tha mínoome edhó mía méra

– a week
Θα μείνουμε εδώ μία εβδομάδα
tha mínoome edhó mía evdhomádha

We're interested in...
Ενδιαφερόμαστε για...
endhiaferómaste ya ...

Is there a scenic walk around the city?
Μπορούμε να κάνουμε μια βόλτα στην πόλη;
boróome na kánoome mya vólta stimbóli?

How long does it take?
Πόσο κρατάει;
póso kratái?

Where does it start/end?
Πού είναι η αφετηρία/το τέρμα;
poo íne i afetería/to térma?

Are there any boat cruises here?
Υπάρχουν εδώ εκδρομικά καραβάκια;
ipárchoon edhó ekdhromiká karavákya?

Where can we board?
Πού μπορούμε να μπαρκάρουμε;
poo boróome na barkároome?

Are there any bus tours?
Γίνονται εκδρομές με πούλμαν;
yínonde ekdhromés me póolman?

Where do we get on?
Πού πρέπει να ανεβούμε;
poo prépi na anevóome?

Is there a guide who speaks English?
Υπάρχει ένας ξεναγός με αγγλικά;
ipárchi énas xenaghós me angliká?

What trips can we take around the area?
Τί εκδρομές μπορεί να κάνει κανείς σ' αυτή την περιοχή;
ti ekdhromés borí na káni avtí timberiohí?

Are there any excursions?
Υπάρχουν οργανωμένες εκδρομές;
ipárchoon orghanoménes ekdhromés?

Where do they go to?
Για πού;
ya poo?

We'd like to go to...
Θέλουμε να πάμε σε...
théloome na páme se ...

How long is the trip?
Πόσο κρατάει αυτή η διαδρομή;
póso kratái aftí i dhiadromí?

How long do we stay in...?	Πόση ώρα θα μείνουμε σε... *pósi óra tha mínoome se ...?*
Are there any guided tours?	Γίνονται ξεναγήσεις εκεί; *yínonde xenayísis ekí?*
How much free time will we have there?	Πόση ώρα θα έχουμε στη διάθεσή μας εκεί; *pósi óra tha échoome sti dhiáthesímas ekí?*
We want to go hiking	Θέλουμε να κάνουμε πεζοπορία *théloome na kánoome pezoporía*
Can we hire a guide?	Μπορούμε να νοικιάσουμε έναν ξεναγό; *boróome na nikyásoome énan xenaghó?*
Can I book mountain huts?	Μπορώ να κλείσω ένα ορειβατικό καταφύγιο; *boró na klíso éna orivatikó katafíyo?*
What time does... open/close?	Τί ώρα ανοίγει/κλείνει το...; *to óra aníyi/klíni to...?*
What days is...open/ closed?	Ποιές μέρες είναι ανοιχτό/κλειστό το...; *pyes méres íne anichtó/klistó to ...?*
What's the admission price?	Πόσο κοστίζει η είσοδος; *póso kostízi i ísodhos?*
Is there a group discount?	Κάνετε έκπτωση για γκρουπ; *kánete ékptosi ya groop?*
Is there a child discount?	Κάνετε έκπτωση για παιδιά; *kánete ékptosi ya pedhyá?*
Is there a discount for pensioners?	Κάνετε έκπτωση για ηλικιωμένους; *kánete ékptosi ya ilikyoménoos?*
Can I take (flash) photos/can I film here?	Επιτρέπεται εδώ η φωτογράφηση (με φλας)/η κινηματογράφηση; *epitrépete edhó i fotoghráfisi (me flash)/i kinimatoghráfisi?*
Do you have any postcards of...?	Πουλάτε κάρτες με...; *pooláte kártes me ...?*
Do you have an English...?	Έχετε ένα ... στα αγγλικά; *éhete éna ... sta angliká?*
– an English catalogue?	Έχετε ένα κατάλογο στα αγγλικά; *éhete éna katálogho sta angliká?*
– an English programme?	Έχετε ένα πρόγραμμα στα αγγλικά; *éhete éna próghrama sta angliká?*
– an English brochure?	Έχετε ένα φυλλάδιο στα αγγλικά; *éhete éna filádhio sta angliká?*

11 .2 Going out

● **In Greece theatres** and cinemas are usually open-air in the summer. Theatre performances usually start at 8.30pm in winter, but later in summer. Cinemas show films between approximately 1.30 and 11pm.

Do you have this week's/month's entertainment guide?	Έχετε το Αθηνόραμα αυτής της εβδομάδας/αυτού του μήνα; *éhete to athinórama aftís tis evdhomádhas/aftóo too mína?*
What's on tonight?	Τί μπορούμε να κάνουμε απόψε; *ti boróome na kánoome apópse?*
We want to go to...	Θέλουμε να πάμε σε... *théloome na páme se ...*

90

Which films are showing? _	Ποιές ταινίες παίζονται τώρα; *pyes teníes pézonde tóra?*
What sort of film is that?___	Τί είδος ταινία είναι αυτή; *ti ídhos tenía íne aftí?*
suitable for _____ the whole family	για όλες τις ηλικίες *ya óles tis ilikíes*
not suitable for_____ children	άνω των 12/16 χρονών *áno ton dhódheka me dekaéxi chronón*
original version _____	πρωτότυπη έκδοση *protótipi ékdhosi*
subtitled _____	με υπότιτλους *me ipotítloos*
dubbed_____	ντουμπλαρισμένη *dooblarizméni*
Is it a continuous_____ showing?	Είναι παράσταση χωρίς διάλειμμα; *íne parástasi chorís dhiálima?*
What's on at...? _____	Τί παίζουν στο... *ti pézoon sto...*
– the theatre? _____	Τί παίζουν στο θέατρο; *ti pézoon sto théatro?*
– the concert hall?_____	Τί παίζουν στην αίθουσα συναυλιών; *ti pézoon stin éthoosa sinavlyón?*
– the opera? _____	Τί παίζουν στην όπερα; *ti pézoon stin ópera?*
Where can I find a good ___ disco around here?	Έχει εδώ κοντά καμμιά καλή ντίσκο; *éhi edhó kondá kamyá kalí dísko?*
Is it members only? _____	Πρέπει να είσαι μέλος; *prépi na íse mélos?*
Where can I find a good ___ nightclub around here?	Έχει εδώ κοντά κανένα καλό νυχτερινό κέντρο; *éhi edhó kondá kanéna kaló nichterinó kéndro?*
Is it evening wear only? ___	Είναι υποχρεωτική η βραδινή ενδυμασία; *íne ipochreotikí i vradhiní endhimasía?*
Should I/we wear _____ formal dress?	Ενδείκνυται η βραδινή ενδυμασία; *endhikníete i vradhiní endhimasía?*
What time does the _____ show start?	Τί ώρα αρχίζει η παράσταση; *ti óra archízi i parástasi?*
When's the next soccer ____ match?	Πότε θα γίνει ο επόμενος ποδοσφαιρικός αγώνας; *póte tha yíni o epómenos podhosferikós aghónas?*
Who's playing?_____	Ποιές ομάδες παίζουν; *pyes omádhes pézoon?*

I'd like an escort for _____
  tonight. Could you arrange
  that for me?
	Θέλω για απόψε ένα/μία έσκορτ. Μπορείτε
	να μου το κανονίσετε;
	*thélo ya apópse éna/mía éskort. boríte na
	moo to kanonísete?*

11

11.3 Booking tickets

Could you book some _____ tickets for us?	Μπορείτε να μας κλείσετε εισιτήρια; *boríte na mas klísete isitírya?*
We'd like to book... _____ seats/a table...	Θέλουμε...θέσεις/ένα τραπέζι *théloome...thésis/éna trapézi*
– in the stalls _____	Θέλουμε...θέσεις στην πλατεία *théloome...thésis stimblatía*
– on the balcony _____	Θέλουμε...θέσεις στον εξώστη *théloome...thésis ston exósti*
– box seats _____	Θέλουμε...θέσεις στο θεωρείο *théloome...thésis sto theorío*
– a table at the front _____	Θέλουμε...θέσεις/ένα τραπέζι μπροστά *théloome...thésis/éna trapézi brostá*
– in the middle _____	Θέλουμε...θέσεις/ένα τραπέζι στη μέση *théloome...thésis/éna trapézi sti mési*
– at the back _____	Θέλουμε...θέσεις/ένα τραπέζι πίσω *théloome...thésis/éna trapézi píso*
Could I book...seats for _____ the...o'clock performance?	Μπορώ να κλείσω...θέσεις για την παράσταση στις...; *boró na klíso...thésis ya timbarástasi stis...?*
Are there any seats left _____ for tonight?	Υπάρχουν ακόμα εισιτήρια για απόψε; *ipárchoon akóma isitírya ya apópse?*
How much is a ticket? _____	Πόσο κοστίζει το εισιτήριο; *póso kostízi to isitíryo?*
When can I pick the _____ tickets up?	Πότε μπορώ να πάρω τα εισιτήρια; *póte boró na páro ta isitírya?*
I've got a reservation _____	Έχω κλείσει θέσεις *écho klísi thésis*
My name's... _____	Το όνομά μου είναι... *to ónomámoo íne...*

Για ποιά παράσταση θέλετε να _____ κλείσετε εισιτήρια;	Which performance do you want to book for?
Πού θέλετε να καθίσετε; _____	Where would you like to sit?
Όλα πουλήθηκαν _____	Everything's sold out
Υπάρχουν μόνο θέσεις για όρθιους _____	It's standing room only
Υπάρχουν μόνο θέσεις στον εξώστη _____	We've only got balcony seats left
Υπάρχουν μόνο θέσεις στη γαλαρία _____	We've only got seats left in the gallery
Υπάρχουν μόνο θέσεις στην πλατεία _____	We've only got stalls seats left
Υπάρχουν μόνο θέσεις μπροστά _____	We've only got seats left at the front
Υπάρχουν μόνο θέσεις πίσω _____	We've only got seats left at the back
Πόσες θέσεις θέλετε; _____	How many seats would you like?
Πρέπει να πάρετε τα εισιτήρια πριν _____ από τις...	You'll have to pick up the tickets before...o'clock
Τα εισιτήριά σας, παρακαλώ _____	Tickets, please
Ορίστε, η θέση σας _____	This is your seat

Sports

Sports

12.1 Sporting questions

Where can we... _____ around here?	Πού μπορούμε να...εδώ; *poo boróome na...edhó?*
Is there a..._____ around here?	Υπάρχει ένα...εδώ κοντά; *ipárchi éna...edhó kondá?*
Can I hire a...here? _____	Μπορώ να νοικιάσω ένα...; *boró na nikyáso éna...?*
Can I take...lessons? _____	Γίνονται μαθήματα...; *yínonde mathímata...?*
How much is that per_____ hour/per day/a turn?	Πόσο κοστίζει την ώρα/τη μέρα/τη φορά; *póso kostízi tin óra/ti méra/ti forá?*
Do I need a permit _____ for that?	Χρειάζομαι μια άδεια για αυτό; *chriázome mya ádhya yavtó?*
Where can I get _____ the permit?	Πού μπορώ να βγάλω μια τέτοια άδεια; *poo boró na vghálo mya tétya ádhya?*

12.2 By the waterfront

Is it a long way to _____ the sea still?	Η θάλασσα είναι ακόμα μακριά; *i thálasa íne akóma makriá?*
Is there a...around here? ___	Υπάρχει κι ένα...εδώ κοντά; *ipárchi kyéna ... edhó kondá?*
– an outdoor/indoor/_____ public swimming pool	Υπάρχει και μια πισίνα εδώ κοντά; *ipárchi ke mya pisína edhó kondá?*
– a sandy beach_____	Υπάρχει και μια παραλία εδώ κοντά; *ipárchi ke mya paralía edhó kondá?*
– a nudist beach_____	Υπάρχει και μια πλαζ για γυμνιστές εδώ κοντά; *ipárchi ke mya plaz ya yimnastés edhó kondá?*
– mooring _____	Υπάρχει και μια μαρίνα εδώ κοντά; *ipárchi ke mya marína edhó kondá?*
Are there any rocks_____ here?	Έχει και βράχους εδώ; *éhi ke vráchoos edhó?*
When's high/low tide? _____	Τί ώρα έχει παλίρροια/άμπωτη; *ti óra éhi palíria/ámboti?*
What's the water _____ temperature?	Τί θερμοκρασία έχει το νερό; *ti thermokrasía éhi to neró?*
Is it (very) deep here? _____	Είναι (πολύ) βαθιά εδώ; *íne (polí) vathyá edhó?*
Can you stand here?_____	Πατώνεις εδώ; *patónis edhó?*
Is it safe (for children) _____ to swim here?	Είναι ασφαλές το κολύμπι εδώ (για παιδιά); *íne asfalés to kolímbi edhó (ya pedhyá)?*
Are there any currents?____	Έχει ρεύματα εδώ; *éhi révmata edhó?*
Are there any rapids/ _____ waterfalls in this river?	Αυτό το ποτάμι έχει καταρράχτες; *aftó to potámi éhi kataráchtes?*
What does that flag/_____ buoy mean?	Τί σημαίνει εκείνη η σημαία/σημαδούρα εκεί; *ti siméni ekíni i siméa/simadhóora ekí?*

Is there a lifeguard on duty here? _____	Έχει εδώ κανένα ακτοφύλακα που να προσέχει;
	éhi edhó kanéna aktofílaka poo na proséhi?
Are dogs allowed here?____	Επιτρέπονται εδώ τα σκυλιά;
	epitréponde edhó ta skilyá?
Is camping on the beach allowed? _____	Επιτρέπεται η κατασκήνωση εδώ στην παραλία;
	epitrépete i kataskínosi edhó stimbaralía?
Are we allowed to build a fire here? _____	Επιτρέπεται να ανάβει κανείς εδώ φωτιά;
	epitrépete nanávi kanís edhó fotyá?

ΑΠΑΓΟΡΕΥΕΤΑΙ ΤΟ ΚΟΛΥΜΠΙ	ΑΠΑΓΟΡΕΥΕΤΑΙ ΤΟ ΨΑΡΕΜΑ	ΚΙΝΔΥΝΟΣ danger
no swimming	no fishing	ΜΟΝΟ ΜΕ ΑΔΕΙΑ
ΑΠΑΓΟΡΕΥΕΤΑΙ ΤΟ ΣΕΡΦΙΝΓΚ	ΕΠΙΤΡΕΠΕΤΑΙ ΤΟ ΨΑΡΕΜΑ	permits only
no surfing	fishing permitted	

12 .3 Water sports

Can I take water-ski lessons here? _____	Μπορώ να κάνω εδώ θαλάσσιο σκι;
	boró na káno edhó thalásyo ski?
Can I get diving instruction here? _____	Μπορώ να κάνω μαθήματα κατάδυσης;
	boró na káno mathímata katadhísis?
How large are the groups? _____	Πόσο μεγάλα είναι τα γκρουπ;
	póso meghála íne ta groop?
What language are the classes in? _____	Σε ποια γλώσσα παραδίνονται τα μαθήματα;
	se pya ghlósa paradhínonde ta mathímata?
Can I hire diving equipment here? _____	Μπορώ να νοικιάσω εδώ εξαρτήματα κατάδυσης;
	boró na nikyáso edhó exartímata katádhisis?
Can I dive here? _____	Μπορώ να κάνω εδώ κατάδυση;
	boró na káno edhó katádhisi?

Sports

12

Sickness

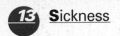

13 Sickness

13.1 Call (fetch) the doctor

Could you call/fetch a _____ doctor quickly, please?	Παρακαλώ, καλέστε/ειδοποιήστε γρήγορα ένα γιατρό *parakaló, kaléste/idhopiíste ghríghora éna yatró*
When does the doctor _____ have surgery?	Πότε δέχεται ο γιατρός; *póte dhéchete o yatrós?*
When can the doctor _____ come?	Πότε μπορεί να έρθει ο γιατρός; *póte borí na érthi o yatrós?*
I'd like to make an _____ appointment to see the doctor	Μπορείτε να μου κλείσετε ένα ραντεβού με το γιατρό; *boríte na moo klísete éna randevóo me to yatró?*
I've got an appointment _____ to see the doctor at...	Έχω ένα ραντεβού με το γιατρό στις... *écho éna randevóo me to yatró stis ...*
Which doctor/chemist _____ has night/weekend duty?	Ποιος γιατρός/ποιό φαρμακείο διανυκτερεύει/διανυκτερεύει το Σαββατοκύριακο; *pyos yatrós/pyo farmakío dhianikterévi/dhianikterévi to savatokíryako?*

13.2 Patient's ailments

I don't feel well _____	Δεν αισθάνομαι καλά *dhen esthánome kalá*
I'm dizzy _____	Ζαλίζομαι *zalízome*
– ill _____	Είμαι άρρωστος/άρρωστη *íme árostos/árosti*
– sick _____	Ανακατεύεται το στομάχι μου *anakatévete to stomáchimoo*
I've got a cold _____	Είμαι κρυωμένος/κρυωμένη *íme krioménos/krioméni*
It hurts here _____	Πονάω εδώ *ponáo edhó*
I've been throwing up _____	Έκανα εμετό *ékana emetó*
I've got... _____	Μ' ενοχλεί... *menochlí...*
I'm running a _____ temperature of...degrees	Έχω...βαθμούς πυρετό *écho...vathmóos piretó*
I've been stung by _____ a wasp	Με τσίμπησε μια σφήκα *me tsíbise mya sfíka*
I've been stung by an _____ insect	Με τσίμπησε ένα έντομο *me tsíbise éna éndomo*
I've been bitten by _____ a dog	Με δάγκωσε ένας σκύλος *me dhángose énas skílos*
I've been stung by _____ a jellyfish	Με τσίμπησε μια μέδουσα *me tsímbise mya medhóosa*
I've been bitten by _____ a snake	Με δάγκωσε ένα φίδι *me dhángose éna fídhi*

I've been bitten by an animal	Με δάγκωσε ένα ζώο
	me dhángose éna zó-o
I've cut myself	Κόπηκα
	kópika
I've burned myself	Κάηκα
	káika
I've grazed myself	Γρατσουνίστηκα
	ghratsoonístika
I've had a fall	Έπεσα
	épesa
I've sprained my ankle	Στραμπούληξα τον αστράγαλό μου
	strambóolixa ton astrághalómoo
I've come for the morning-after pill	Έρχομαι για το μόρνιγκ-άφτερ-χάπι
	érchome ya to morning-áfter-chápi

🔵 .3 The consultation

Τί ενοχλήσεις έχετε;	What seems to be the problem?
Από πότε αισθάνεσθε έτσι;	How long have you had these symptoms?
Είχατε και παλαιότερα αυτές τις ενοχλήσεις;	Have you had this trouble before?
Τί πυρετό έχετε;	How high is your temperature?
Γδυθείτε, παρακαλώ	Get undressed, please
Μπορείτε να γδυθείτε μέχρι τη μέση;	Strip to the waist, please
Μπορείτε να γδυθείτε εκεί	You can undress there
Σηκώστε το αριστερό/δεξιό μανίκι σας, παρακαλώ	Roll up your left/right sleeve, please
Ξαπλώστε εκεί	Lie down here, please
Πονάτε εδώ;	Does this hurt?
Αναπνεύστε βαθιά	Breathe deeply
Ανοίξτε το στόμα σας	Open your mouth

Patient's medical history

I'm a diabetic	Είμαι διαβητικός
	íme dhiavitikós
I have a heart condition	Είμαι καρδιακός
	íme kardhiakós
I have asthma	Έχω άσθμα
	écho ásthma
I'm allergic to...	Είμαι αλλεργικός σε...
	íme aleryikós se...
I'm...months pregnant	Είμαι...μηνών έγκυος
	íme...minón éngios
I'm on a diet	Κάνω δίαιτα
	káno dhíeta

I'm on medication/the pill __	Παίρνω φάρμακα/το χάπι *pérno fármaka/to chápi*
I've had a heart attack ____ once before	Έχω ξαναπάθει καρδιακή προσβολή *écho xanapáthi kardhiakí prosvolí*
I've had a(n)...operation ___	Έκανα εγχείρηση στο... *ékana enchírisi sto...*
I've been ill recently _____	Πρόσφατα ήμουν άρρωστος/άρρωστη *prósfata ímoon árostos/árosti*
I've got an ulcer_____	Έχω στομαχικό έλκος *écho stomachikó élkos*
I've got my period_____	Έχω περίοδο *écho períodho*

Είστε αλλεργικός σε κάτι; _____	Do you have any allergies?
Παίρνετε φάρμακα _____	Are you on any medication?
Κάνετε δίαιτα; _____	Are you on a diet?
Είστε έγκυος; _____	Are you pregnant?
Είστε εμβολιασμένος _____ κατά του τέτανου...;	Have you had a tetanus injection?

The diagnosis

Δεν είναι τίποτα σοβαρό_____	It's nothing serious
Έχετε σπάσει...το/τη...σας _____	Your...is broken
Έχετε στραμπουλήξει...το/τη...σας_____	You've got a strained/sprained...
Έχετε σκίσει...το/τη...σας _____	You've got (a) torn...
Έχετε μια φλεγμονή _____	You've got an inflammation
Έχετε σκωληκοειδίτιδα_____	You've got appendicitis
Έχετε βρογχίτιδα _____	You've got bronchitis
Έχετε ένα αφροδίσιο νόσημα _____	You've got a venereal disease
Έχετε γρίππη_____	You've got the flu
Πάθατε καρδιακή προσβολή _____	You've had a heart attack
Έχετε ίωση/βακτηριακή μόλυνση _____	You've got an infection (viral..., bacterial...)
Έχετε πνευμονία _____	You've got pneumonia
Έχετε έλκος _____	You've got an ulcer
Έχετε πάθει νευροκαβαλίκεμα _____	You've pulled a muscle
Έχετε κολπική μόλυνση _____	You've got a vaginal infection
Πάθατε τροφική δηλητηρίαση_____	You've got food poisoning
Έχετε πάθει ηλίαση_____	You've got sunstroke
Είστε αλλεργικός στο/στη... _____	You're allergic to...
Είστε έγκυος _____	You're pregnant
Θέλω να κάνω εξέταση του αίματός _____ σας/των ούρων σας/των κοπράνων σας	I'd like to have your blood/urine/stools tested

Πρέπει να ραφτεί _____	It needs stitching
Σας στέλνω σ' ένα ειδικό/σ' ένα _____ νοσοκομείο	I'm referring you to a specialist/sending you to hospital
Πρέπει να κάνουμε ακτινογραφίες_____	You'll need to have some x-rays taken
Πρέπει να περιμένετε δύο _____ λεπτά στην αίθουσα αναμονής	Could you wait in the waiting room, please?
Πρέπει να εγχειρισθείτε _____	You'll need an operation

Is it contagious?_____ Είναι κολλητικό;
íne kolitikó?

How long do I have to _____ Πόσο καιρό πρέπει να μείνω σε...;
stay...? *póso kyeró prépi na míno se...?*

– in bed _____ Πόσο καιρό πρέπει να μείνω στο κρεβάτι;
póso kyeró prépi na míno sto kreváti?

– in hospital _____ Πόσο καιρό πρέπει να μείνω στο
νοσοκομείο;
póso kyeró prépi na míno sto nosokomío?

Do I have to go on _____ Πρέπει να κάνω καμιά δίαιτα;
a special diet? *prépi na káno kamyá dhíeta?*

Am I allowed to travel? ____ Μπορώ να ταξιδέψω;
boró na taxidhépso?

Can I make a new _____ Μπορώ να κλείσω ένα άλλο ραντεβού;
appointment? *boró na klíso éna álo randevóo?*

When do I have to_____ Πότε πρέπει να ξανάρθω;
come back? *póte prépi na xanártho?*

I'll come back _____ Θα ξανάρθω αύριο
tomorrow *tha xanártho ávrio*

Πρέπει να ξαναρθείτε αύριο/σε...μέρες ____ Come back
tomorrow/in...days' time

13.4 Medication and prescriptions

How do I take this _____ Πώς πρέπει να το παίρνω αυτό το φάρμακο;
medicine? *pos prépi na to pérno aftó to fármako?*

How many capsules/ _____ Πόσες κάψουλες/σταγόνες/ενέσεις/πόσα
drops/injections/spoonfuls/ κουταλάκια/χάπια τη φορά;
tablets each time? *póses kapsóoles/staghónes/enésis/pósa
kootalákya/chápya ti forá?*

How many times a day? ___ Πόσες φορές την ημέρα;
póses forés tin iméra?

I've forgotten my_____ Ξέχασα τα φάρμακά μου. Σπίτι χρησιμοποιώ...
medication. At home I *xéchasa ta fármakámoo. spíti chrisimopió ...*
take...

Could you make out a _____ Μπορείτε να μου δώσετε μια συνταγή;
prescription for me? *boríte na moo dhósete mya sintayí?*

Θα σας δώσω αντιβιοτικά/ένα σιρόπι/ ____ εναηρεμιστικό/ένα παυσίπονο	I'm prescribing antibiotics/a mixture/a tranquillizer/painkillers
Πρέπει να ξεκουραστείτε _____	Have lots of rest
Καλύτερα να μην βγείτε έξω _____	Stay indoors
Πρέπει να μείνετε στο κρεβάτι_____	Stay in bed

αλείφω	κατά τη διάρκεια...	παίρνω
rub on	ημερών	take
αλοιφή	for...days	πριν από κάθε
ointment	καταπίνω ολόκληρο	γεύμα
αυτά τα φάρμακα	swallow whole	before every meal
επηρεάζουν την	κάψουλες	σταγόνες
ικανότητα οδήγησης	capsules	drops
this medication	κουτάλια/κουταλάκια	τελειώνω τη θεραπεία
impairs your	spoonfuls	finish the course
driving	(tablespoons/	of treatment
διαλύω σε νερό	teaspoons)	...φορές το
dissolve in water	μόνο για εξωτερική	μερόνυχτο
ενέσεις	χρήση	...times a day
injections	not for internal	χάπια
κάθε...ώρες	use	pills
every...hours		

🕙 .5 At the dentist's

Do you know a good _____ dentist?	Ξέρετε ένα καλό οδοντογιατρό; *xérete éna kaló odhondoyatró?*
Could you make a _____ dentist's appointment for me? It's urgent	Μπορείτε να μου κλείσετε ραντεβού με τον οδοντογιατρό; Είναι επείγον *boríte na moo klísete randevóo me ton odhondoyatró? íne epíghon*
Can I come in today,_____ please?	Μπορώ να έρθω σήμερα, παρακαλώ; *boró na értho símera, parakaló?*
I have (terrible)_____ toothache	Έχω (φοβερό) πονόδοντο *écho (foveró) ponódhondo*
Could you prescribe/ _____ give me a painkiller?	Μπορείτε να μου γράψετε/δώσετε ένα παυσίπονο; *boríte na moo ghrápsete/dhósete éna pafsípono?*
A piece of my tooth _____ has broken off	Έσπασε ένα κομματάκι του δοντιού μου/του τραπεζίτη μου *éspase éna komatáki too dondyóomoo/too trapezítimoo*
My filling's come out _____	Βγήκε ένα σφράγισμα *vyíke éna sfráyizma*
I've got a broken crown____	Έσπασε η κορόνα μου *éspase i koróna moo*
I'd like/I don't want a _____ local anaesthetic	Θέλω/δε θέλω τοπική αναισθησία *thélo/dhe thélo topikí anesthisía*

Sickness

13

Can you do a makeshift____ Μπορείτε να με βοηθήσετε προσωρινά;
repair job? *boríte na me voithísete prosoriná?*

I don't want this tooth ____ Δε θέλω να το βγάλετε αυτόν τον
pulled τραπεζίτη
dhe thélo na to vghálete aftón ton trapezíti

My dentures are broken. __ Η μασέλα μου έσπασε. Μπορείτε να τη
Can you fix them? φτιάξετε;
i masélamoo éspase. boríte na ti ftyáxete?

Ποιό δόντι/ποιός τραπεζίτης σας _____ Which tooth/molar hurts?
πονάει;

Έχετε ένα απόστημα _____ You've got an abscess

Πρέπει να κάνω απονεύρωση _____ I'll have to do a root canal

Θα σας κάνω τοπική αναισθησία _____ I'm giving you a local
anaesthetic

Πρέπει να βουλώσω/βγάλω/λιμάρω_____ I'll have to fill/pull/file this
αυτό το δόντι tooth down

Πρέπει να τρυπήσω το δόντι _____ I'll have to drill

Ανοίξτε το στόμα _____ Open wide, please

Κλείστε το στόμα _____ Close your mouth, please

Ξεπλύντε το _____ Rinse, please

Πονάει ακόμα; _____ Does it hurt still?

In trouble

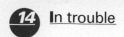

14 In trouble

14.1 Asking for help

Help!	Βοήθεια! *voíthya!*
Fire!	Φωτιά! *fotyá!*
Police!	Αστυνομία! *astinomía!*
Quick!	Γρήγορα! *ghríghora!*
Danger!	Κίνδυνος! *kíndhinos!*
Watch out!	Προσοχή! *prosohí!*
Stop!	Σταματήστε! *stamatíste!*
Be careful!	Προσοχή! *prosohí!*
Don't!	Μή! *mi!*
Let go!	Άφήστέ το! *afiséto*
Stop that thief!	Πιάστε τον κλέφτη! *pyáste tongléfti!*
Could you help me, please?	Μπορείτε να με βοηθήσετε; *boríte na me voithísete?*
Where's the police station/emergency exit/fire escape?	Πού είναι το αστυνομικό τμήμα/η έξοδος κινδύνου/η σκάλα πυρκαγιάς; *poo íne to astinomikó tmíma/i exodhos kindhínoo/i skála pirkayas?*
Where's the nearest fire extinguisher?	Πού βρίσκεται ένας πυροσβεστήρας; *poo vrískete énas pirosvestíras?*
Call the fire brigade!	Ειδοποιείστε την πυροσβεστική υπηρεσία! *idhopiíste timbirosvestikí ipiresía!*
Call the police!	Τηλεφωνήστε στην αστυνομία! *tilefoníste stin astinomía!*
Call an ambulance!	Ειδοποιήστε ένα ασθενοφόρο! *idhopiíste éna asthenofóro!*
Where's the nearest phone?	Πού υπάρχει ένα τηλέφωνο; *poo ipárchi éna tiléfono?*
Could I use your phone?	Μπορώ να χρησιμοποιήσω το τηλέφωνό σας; *boró na chrisimopiíso to tiléfonósas?*
What's the emergency number?	Ποιός είναι ο αριθμός του συναγερμού; *pyos íne o arithmós too sinayermóo?*
What's the number for the police?	Ποιός είναι ο αριθμός της αστυνομίας; *pyos íne o arithmós tis astinomías?*

In trouble

14

14.2 Loss

I've lost my purse/ _____ Έχασα το πορτοφόλι μου
 wallet *échasa to portofólimoo*

I lost my...yesterday _____ Ξέχασα χτες το...μου
 xéchasa chtes to...moo

I left my...here _____ Άφησα εδώ το...μου
 áfisa edhó to...moo

Did you find my...? _____ Μήπως βρήκατε το...μου;
 mípos vríkate to...moo?

It was right here _____ Ήταν εδώ
 tan edhó

It's quite valuable _____ Είναι πολύτιμο
 íne polítimo

Where's the lost _____ Πού βρίσκεται το γραφείο ευρεθέντων
 property office? αντικειμένων;
 *poo vrískete to ghrafío evrethéndon
 andikiménon?*

14.3 Accidents

There's been an accident __ Έγινε ένα ατύχημα
 éyine éna atíhima

Someone's fallen into _____ Κάποιος έπεσε στο νερό
 the water *kápyos épese sto neró*

There's a fire _____ Ξέσπασε πυρκαγιά
 xéspase pirkayá

Is anyone hurt? _____ Υπάρχουν τραυματίες;
 ipárchoon travmatíes?

Some people have _____ (Δεν) υπάρχουν τραυματίες
 been/no one's been *(dhen) ipárchoon travmatíes*
 injured

There's someone in _____ Έχει και άλλον έναν στο αυτοκίνητο/στο
 the car/train still τρένο
 éhi ke álo énan sto aftokínito/sto tréno

It's not too bad. Don't _____ Δεν είναι και τόσο άσχημα. Μην ανησυχείτε
 worry *dhen íne ke tóso áschima. min anisihíte*

Leave everything the _____ Μην κουνήσετε τίποτα
 way it is, please *min koonísete típota*

I want to talk to the _____ Θέλω πρώτα να μιλήσω με την αστυνομία
 police first *thélo próta na milíso me tin astinomía*

I want to take a _____ Θέλω πρώτα να βγάλω μία φωτογραφία
 photo first *thélo próta na vghálo mya fotoghrafía*

Here's my name _____ Να το όνομά μου και η διεύθυνσή μου
 and address *na to ónomámoo ke i dhiéfthinsímoo*

Could I have your _____ Μου δίνετε το όνομά σας και τη διεύθυνσή σας;
 name and address? *moo dhínete to ónomásas ke ti
 dhiéfthinsísas?*

Could I see some _____ Μπορώ να δω την ταυτότητά σας/τα χαρτιά
 identification/your της ασφάλειάς σας;
 insurance papers? *boró na dho tin taftótitásas/ta chartyá tis
 asfalyás sas?*

Will you act as a _____ Θέλετε να εμφανιστείτε ως μάρτυρας;
 witness? *thélete na emfanistíte os mártiras?*

I need the details for _____ Χρειάζομαι τα στοιχεία για την ασφάλεια
 the insurance *chriázome ta stihía ya tin asfálya*

Are you insured? _____	Είστε ασφαλισμένος/ασφαλισμένη;
	íste asfalizménos/asfalizméni?
Third party or _____	Απλή ή μικτή ασφάλεια;
comprehensive?	*aplí i miktí asfálya?*
Could you sign here, _____	Παρακαλώ, να υπογράψετε εδώ
please?	*parakaló, na ipoghrápsete edhó*

🎱 .4 Theft

I've been robbed _____	Μ' έκλεψαν
	méklepsan
My...has been stolen _____	Έκλεψαν το...μου
	éklepsan to...moo
My car's been _____	Παραβίασαν το αυτοκίνητό μου
broken into	*paravíasan to aftokínitómoo*

🎱 .5 Missing person

I've lost my child/ _____	Έχασα το παιδί μου/τη γιαγιά μου
grandmother	*échasa to pedhímoo/ti yayámoo*
Could you help me _____	Μπορείτε να με βοηθήσετε να το/τη βρω;
find him/her?	*boríte na me voithísete na to/ti vro?*
Have you seen a _____	Μήπως είδατε ένα μικρό παιδί;
small child?	*mípos ídhate éna mikró pedhí?*
He's/she's...years old _____	Είναι...χρονών
	íne...chronó
He's/she's got _____	Έχει...κοντά/μακριά/ξανθά/κόκκινα/
short/long/blond/red/	καστανά/μαύρα/γκρίζα/σγουρά/ίσια/
brown/black/grey/curly/	κατσαρά μαλλιά
straight/frizzy hair	*éhi kondá/makryá/xanthá/kókina/kastaná/*
	mávra/gríza/zghoorá/ ísya/ katsará malyá
with a ponytail _____	με αλογοουρά
	me aloghó-oorá
with plaits _____	με κοτσίδες
	me kotsídhes
in a bun _____	με κότσο
	me kótso
He's/she's got _____	Τα μάτια του/της είναι
blue/brown/green eyes	μπλε/καστανά/πράσινα
	ta mátya too/tis íne ble/kastaná/prásina
He's wearing swimming ___	Φοράει μαγιό/παπούτσια ορειβασίας
trunks/mountaineering	*forái mayó/papóotsya orivalsaís*
boots	
with/without glasses/ _____	με/χωρίς γυαλιά/τσάντα
a bag	*me/chorís yalyá/tsánda*
tall/short _____	ψηλός/κοντός
	psilós/kondós
This is a photo of _____	Να μια φωτογραφία του/της
him/her	*na mya fotoghrafía too/tis*
He/she must be lost _____	Μάλλον έχασε το δρόμο
	málon échase to dhrómo

An arrest

Τα χαρτιά του αυτοκινήτου σας, παρακαλώ _____	Your registration papers, please
Τρέχατε πολύ _____	You were speeding
Παρκάρατε παράνομα _____	You're not allowed to park here
Δε βάλατε λεφτά στο παρκόμετρο _____	You haven't put money in the meter
Τα φώτα σας δε λειτουργούν _____	Your lights aren't working
Θα πληρώσετε πρόστιμο ... δραχμών _____	That's a...drachma fine
Θέλετε να πληρώσετε αμέσως; _____	Do you want to pay on the spot?
Πρέπει να πληρώσετε αμέσως _____	You'll have to pay on the spot

I don't speak Greek _____	Δε μιλάω ελληνικά
	dhe miláo eliniká
I didn't see the sign _____	Δεν είδα εκείνη την πινακίδα
	dhen ídha ekíni timbinakídha
I don't understand _____ what it says	Δεν καταλαβαίνω τι λέει εδώ
	dhengkatalavéno ti léi edhó
I was only doing... _____ kilometres an hour	Οδηγούσα μόνο ... χιλιόμετρα την ώρα
	odhighóosa móno ... hilyómetra tin óra
I'll have my car checked ___	Θα πάω το αυτοκίνητό μου στο συνεργείο
	tha páo to aftokínitómoo sto sineryío
I was blinded by _____ oncoming lights	Τυφλώθηκα από ένα αυτοκίνητο που ερχόταν από την αντίθετη κατεύθυνση
	tiflóthika apó éna aftokínito poo erchótan apó tin andítheti katéfthinsi

At the police station

I want to report a _____ collision/missing person/rape	Ήρθα για να αναφέρω μια σύγκρουση/μια απώλεια/ένα βιασμό
	írtha ya na anféro mya síngroosi/mya apólya/éna viazmó
Could you make out _____ a report, please?	Μπορείτε να κάνετε αναφορά για το αυτόφωρο;
	boríte na kánete anaforá ya to aftóforo?
Could I have a copy _____ for the insurance?	Μπορείτε να μου δώσετε ένα αντίγραφο για την ασφάλεια;
	boríte na moo dhósete éna andíghrafo ya tin asfálya?
I've lost everything _____	Έχασα τα πάντα
	échasa ta pánda
I've no money; I don't _____ know what to do	Τα λεφτά μου τελείωσαν, δεν ξέρω τί να κάνω
	ta leftámoo telíosan, dhengkséro ti na káno
Could you lend me a _____ little cash?	Μπορείτε να μου δανείσετε λίγα λεφτά;
	boríte na moo dhanísete lígha leftá?

In trouble

14

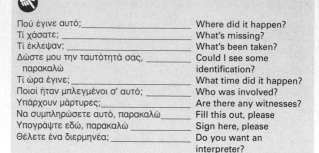

Πού έγινε αυτό; _____	Where did it happen?
Τί χάσατε; _____	What's missing?
Τί έκλεψαν; _____	What's been taken?
Δώστε μου την ταυτότητά σας, _____ παρακαλώ	Could I see some identification?
Τί ώρα έγινε; _____	What time did it happen?
Ποιοί ήταν μπλεγμένοι σ' αυτό; _____	Who was involved?
Υπάρχουν μάρτυρες; _____	Are there any witnesses?
Να συμπληρώσετε αυτό, παρακαλώ _____	Fill this out, please
Υπογράψτε εδώ, παρακαλώ _____	Sign here, please
Θέλετε ένα διερμηνέα; _____	Do you want an interpreter?

I'd like an interpreter _____ Θα ήθελα ένα διερμηνέα
tha íthela éna dhierminéa

I'm innocent _____ Είμαι αθώος
íme athó-os

I don't know anything _____ Δεν ξέρω τίποτα για αυτό
about it *dhengxéro típota yaftó*

I want to speak to _____ Θέλω να μιλήσω με κάποιον από ...
someone from... *thélo na milíso me kápyon apó ...*

I want to speak to _____ Θέλω να μιλήσω με κάποιον από το
someone from the British βρεττανικό προξενείο
consulate *thélo na milíso me kápyon apó to vretanikó proxenío*

I need to see someone _____ Θέλω να μιλήσω με κάποιον από τη
from the British embassy βρεττανική πρεσβεία
thélo na milíso me kápyon apó ti vretanikí prezvía

I want a lawyer who _____ Θέλω ένα δικηγόρο που να μιλάει αγγλικά
speaks English *thélo éna dhikighóro poo na milái angliká*

4 In trouble

Word list

Word list English - Greek

● **This word list** is intended to supplement the previous chapters. Nouns are usually accompanied by the Greek definite article in order to indicate whether the word is masculine (o), feminine (η), or neuter (το). In the case of a plural noun the form of the definite article will be οι for masculine and feminine nouns and τα for neuter nouns.

In a number of cases, words not contained in this list can be found elsewhere in this book, namely alongside the diagrams of the car, the bicycle and the tent. Many food terms can be found in the Greek-English list in 4.7.

A

a little	λίγο	lígho
about	περίπου	perípoo
above	πάνω	páno
abroad	το εξωτερικό	to exoterikó
accident	το ατύχημα	to atíhima
according	κατά	katá
adder	η οχιά	i ochyá
addition	η πρόσθεση	i prósthesi
address	η διεύθυνση	i dhiéfthinsi
admission	η είσοδος	i ísodhos
admission price	η είσοδος	i ísodhos
adult	μεγάλος	meghálos
advice	η συμβουλή	i simvoolí
afraid (I am)	φοβάμαι	fováme
after, afterwards	μετά	metá
aftershave	το αφτερ-σέιβ	to áfter-séiv
afternoon	το απόγευμα	to apóyevma
again	ξανά	xaná
against	ενάντια σε	enándya se
age	η ηλικία	i ilikía
AIDS	ΕΙΤΖ	éitz
air mattress	το αερόστρωμα	to aeróstroma
air-conditioning	ο κλιματισμός	o klimatizmós
aircraft	το αεροπλάνο	to aeropláno
airport	το αεροδρόμιο	to aerodhrómio
airsickness bag	η σακούλα για εμετό	i sakóola ya emetó
alarm	ο συναγερμός	o sinayermós
alarm clock	το ξυπνητήρι	to xipnitíri
alcohol	το αλκοόλ	to alkoól
allergic	αλλεργικός	aleryikós
alone/only	μόνος	mónos
alter	αλλάζω	alázo
always	πάντα	pánda
ambulance	το ασθενοφόρο	to asthenofóro
amount	το ποσό	to posó
amusement park	το λούνα παρκ	to lóonapark
anaesthetize	ναρκώνω	narkóno
anchovy	η αντσούγια	i antsóoya
ancient/very old	αρχαίος	archéos
angry	θυμωμένος	thimoménos
animal	το ζώο	to zóo
ankle	ο αστράγαλος	o astrághalos
answer	η απάντηση	i apándisi
ant	το μυρμήγκι	to mirmíngi

antibiotics	τα αντιβιοτικά	*ta andiviotiká*
antifreeze	το αντιψυκτικό	*to andipsiktikó*
antique (an)	η αντίκα	*i antíka*
anus	ο πρωκτός	*o proktós*
apartment	το διαμέρισμα	*to dhiamérizma*
apologies	συγγνώμη	*sighnómi*
appetiser	το ορεκτικό	*to orektikó*
apple juice	ο χυμός μήλων	*o himós mílon*
apple	το μήλο	*to mílo*
apple sauce	ο πολτός μήλων	*o poltós mílon*
apple pie	η μηλόπιτα	*i milópita*
appointment/date	το ραντεβού	*to randevóo*
apricot	το βερίκοκο	*to veríkoko*
April	ο Απρίλιος	*o aprílios*
archbishop	ο αρχιεπίσκοπος	*o archiepískopos*
architecture	η αρχιτεκτονική	*i architektonikí*
arm	το χέρι	*to héri*
arrive	φτάνω	*ftáno*
arrow	το βέλος	*to vélos*
art	η τέχνη	*i téchni*
artery	η αρτηρία	*i artiría*
artichokes	οι αγγινάρες	*i angináres*
artificial	η τεχνητή αναπνοή	*i technití anapnoí*
ashtray	το τασάκι	*to tasáki*
ask (for)	ζητώ	*zitó*
ask (question)	ρωτάω	*rotáo*
asparagus	τα σπαράγγια	*ta sparángya*
aspirin	η ασπιρίνη	*i aspiríni*
at home	σπίτι	*spíti*
aubergine	η μελιτζάνα	*i melitzána*
August	ο Αύγουστος	*o ávghoostos*
automatic (adj.)	αυτόματος	*aftómatos*
automatic (noun)	το αυτόματο	*to aftómato*
autumn	το φθινόπωρο	*to fthinóporo*
awake	ξύπνιος	*xípnios*
awning	το αλεξήλιο	*to alexílyo*

B

baby food	το φαγητό για μωρά	*to fayitó ya morá*
baby	το μωρό	*to moró*
baby's bottle	το μπιμπερό	*to biberó*
babysitter	η μπέιμπυ σίτερ	*i béibi-síter*
bachelor	ο εργένης	*o eryénis*
back	η πλάτη	*i pláti*
back, at the	πίσω	*píso*
backpack	ο σάκος	*o sákos*
bacterial infection	η βακτηριακή μόλυνση	*i vaktiriakí mólinsi*
bad (serious)	σοβαρός	*sovarós*
bad	κακός	*kakós*
bakery	το αρτοπωλείο/ο φούρνος	*to artopolío/o fóornos*
balcony (in theatre)	ο εξώστης	*o exóstis*
balcony	το μπαλκόνι	*to balkóni*
ball	η μπάλα	*i bála*
ballet	το μπαλέτο	*to baléto*
banana	η μπανάνα	*i banána*
bandage	ο επίδεσμος	*o epídhezmos*

bank	η τράπεζα	i trápeza
bank card	η τραπεζική κάρτα	i trapezikí kárta
bank (river)	η όχθη	i óchthi
bar (café)	το μπαρ	to bar
bar (drink's cabinet)	το μπαρ	to bar
barbecue	το μπαρμπεκιού	to barbekyóo
barber	ο κουρέας	o kooréas
basketball	το μπάσκετ	to básket
bath/swim	το μπάνιο	to bányo
bath foam	το αφρόλουτρο μπάνιου	to afrólootro bányoo
bath	το μπάνιο	to bányo
bath towel	η πετσέτα	i petséta
bathing cap	η σκούφια του μπάνιου	i skóofya too bányoo
bathing-hut	η καμπίνα	i kabína
battery	η μπαταρία	i bataría
beach	η πλαζ	i plaz
beans	τα φασόλια	ta fasólya
beautiful	όμορφος	ómorfos
beauty parlour	το ινστιτούτο καλλονής	to institóoto kalonís
bed	το κρεβάτι	to kreváti
bee	η μέλισσα	i mélissa
beef	το βοδινό κρέας	to vodhinó kréas
beer	η μπύρα	i bíra
beetroot	το παντζάρι	to padzári
begin	αρχίζω	archízo
beginner	ο αρχάριος	o archáryos
behind	πίσω από	píso apó
belly	η κοιλιά	i kilyá
belly ache	ο κοιλόπονος	o kilóponos
beloved	αγαπημένος	aghapiménos
belt	η ζώνη	i zóni
bicarbonate of soda	η σόδα	i sódha
bicycle	το ποδήλατο	to podhílato
bicycle pump	η τρόμπα	i trómba
big	μεγάλος	meghálos
bikini	το μπικίνι	to bikíni
bill	ο λογαριασμός	o loghariazmós
billiards	το μπιλιάρδο	to bilyárdho
biro	το στυλό	to stiló
birthday	τα γενέθλια	ta yenéthlia
birthday (it's my)	έχω γενέθλια	écho yenéthlia
biscuits	τα μπισκότα	ta biskóta
bite (verb)	δαγκώνω	dhangóno
bitter (adj.)	πικρός	pikrós
black	μαύρος	mávros
black bread	το μαύρο ψωμί	to mávro psomí
bland	άνοστος	ánostos
blanket	η κουβέρτα	i koovérta
bleach	ξανθαίνω	xanthéno
blister	η φουσκάλα	i fooskála
block of flats	η πολυκατοικία	i polikatikía
blond	ξανθός	xanthós
blood	το αίμα	to éma
blood pressure	η αρτηριακή πίεση	i artiriakí píesi

blouse	η μπλούζα	i blóoza
blow-dry hair	στεγνώνω τα μαλλιά	steghnóno ta malyá
blue	μπλε	ble
boat	το καράβι	to karávi
body lotion	η λοσιόν	i losyón
body	το σώμα	to sóma
boiled	βρασμένος	vrazménos
bone	το κόκαλο	to kókalo
bonnet	το καπό	to kapó
book	το βιβλίο	to vivlío
book (verb)	κλείνω	klíno
bookshop	το βιβλιοπωλείο	to vivliopolío
booked	κρατημένος	kratiménos
borders (of country)	τα σύνορα	ta sínora
bored, I am	βαριέμαι	varyéme
boring	πληκτικός	pliktikós
born	γεννημένος	yeniménos
borrow	δανείζομαι	dhanízome
boss	το αφεντικό	to afendikó
botanical gardens	ο βοτανικός κήπος	o votanikós kípos
both	και οι δύο/και τα δύο	ke i dhío/ke ta dhío
bothers me	μ' ενοχλεί	menochlí
bottle	το μπουκάλι	to bookáli
box (theatre)	το θεωρείο	to theorío
box	το κουτί	to kootí
boy	το αγόρι	to aghóri
bra	το σουτιέν	to sootyén
bracelet	το βραχιόλι	to vrahyóli
braised	βρασμένος	vrazménos
brake	το φρένο	to fréno
brake fluid	το υγρό φρένου	to ighró frénoo
brake oil	το λάδι φρένου	to ládhi frénoo
brandy	το κονιάκ	to konyák
bread	το ψωμί	to psomí
bread-roll	το ψωμάκι	to psomáki
break	σπάζω	spázo
breakfast	το πρωινό	to proinó
breast	στήθος	to stíthos
bridge	η γέφυρα	i yéfira
briefs	το σλιπάκι	to slipáki
bring	φέρνω	férno
brochure	το φυλλάδιο	to filádhyo
broken	σπασμένος, χαλασμένος	spazménos, chalazménos
broth	το ζουμί	to zoomí
brother	ο αδερφός	o adherfós
brown	καστανός	kastanós
brush	βούρτσα	i vóortsa
Brussels sprouts	η λαχανάκια Βρυξελλών	lachanákya vrixelón
bucket	ο κουβάς	o koovás
bugs	τα ζωύφια	ta zoífya
building	το κτίριο	to ktíryo
buoy	η σημαδούρα	i simadhóora
bureau de change	το γραφείο συναλλάγματος	to ghrafío sinalághmatos
burglary	η διάρρηξη	i dhiárixi

Word list

15

burn	το έγκαυμα	to éngkavma
burn (verb)	καίω	kéo
burnt	καμένος	kaménos
bus stop	η στάση	i stási
bus station	ο σταθμός λεωφορείων	o stathmós leoforíon
bus	το λεωφορείο	to leoforío
business class	μπιζνεσκλάς	biznesklás
business trip	η περιοδεία	i perodhía
butane gas	το υγραέριο	to ighraério
butcher	ο χασάπης	o chasápis
butter	το βούτυρο	to vóotiro
button	το κουμπί	to koobí
buy	αγοράζω	aghorázo
by phone	τηλεφωνικώς	tilefonikós
by air	αεροπορικώς	aeroporikós

C

cabbage	το λάχανο	to láchano
cabin	η καμπίνα	i kabína
café	το καφενείο	to kafenío
cake	η πάστα, η τούρτα	i pásta, i tóorta
call (phone)	τηλεφωνώ	tilefonó
camera	η φωτογραφική μηχανή	i fotoghrafikí michaní
camp (verb)	κατασκηνώνω	kataskinóno
camp site	το κάμπινγκ	to kámping
camping van	το κάμπερ	to kámper
camping permit	η άδεια κατασκήνωσης	i ádhya kataskínosis
camping guide	ο κατάλογος κατασκήνωσης	o katáloghos kataskínosis
camping	το κάμπιγκ	to kámping
camping shop	το μαγαζί του κάμπιγκ	to maghazí too kámping
cancel	ακυρώνω	akiróno
candle	το κερί	to kerí
canoe	το κανό	to kanó
canoe (verb)	κάνω κανό	káno kanó
car trouble	η βλάβη	i vlávi
car	το αυτοκίνητο	to aftokínito
car papers	τα χαρτιά του αυτοκινήτου	ta chartyá too aftokinítoo
car park/parking space	το πάρκιγκ	to párking
car-deck	το κατάστρωμα για τα αυτοκίνητα	to katástroma ya ta aftokínita
carafe	η καράφα	i karáfa
caravan	το τροχόσπιτο	to trochóspito
cardigan	η ζακέτα	i zakéta
careful	προσεχτικός	prosechtikós
carriage (of train)	το βαγόνι	to vaghóni
carrot	το καρότο	to karóto
carton	η κούτα	i kóota
cash desk	το ταμείο	to tamío
casino	το καζίνο	to kazíno
cassette/cartridge	η κασέτα	i kaséta
castle	το κάστρο	o kástro
cat	η γάτα	i gháta

catalogue	ο κατάλογος	o katáloghos
cathedral	η μητρόπολη	i mitrópoli
cauliflower	το κουνουπίδι	to koonoopídhi
cave	η σπηλιά	i spilyá
celebrate	γιορτάζω	yortázo
celebration	η γιορτή	i yortí
cemetery	το νεκροταφείο	to nekrotafío
centimetre	ο πόντος	o póndos
centre	το κέντρο	to kéndro
chain	η αλυσίδα	i alisídha
chair	η καρέκλα	i karékla
chalet area	ο χώρος με μπάγκαλοου	o chóros me bángaló-óo
chambermaid	η καμαριέρα	i kamaryéra
champagne	η σαμπάνια	i sampánya
change (verb)	αλλάζω	alázo
change the oil	αλλάζω τα λάδια	alázo ta ládhya
change (small)	τα ψιλά	ta psilá
change (baby's nappy)	καθαρίζω	katharízo
chapel	το εξωκλήσι	to exoklísi
charter flight	η πτήση τσάρτερ	i ptísi-tsárter
chat up someone	ψωνίζω κάποιον	psonízo kápyon
cheap	φτηνός	ftinós
check (verb)	ελέγχω	eléncho
check in	τσεκάρω	tsekáro
cheers	στην υγειά σας	stiniyásas
cheese	το τυρί	to tirí
chemist's	το φαρμακείο	to farmakío
cheque	η επιταγή	i epitayí
cherries	τα κεράσια	ta kerásya
chess	το σκάκι	to skáki
chewing gum	η τσίχλα/η μαστίχα	i tsíchla/i mastícha
chicken	το κοτόπουλο	to kotópoolo
chicory	τα ραδίκια	ta radhíya
child seat (in car)	το παιδικό κάθισμα	to pedhikó káthizma
child	το παιδί	to pedhí
child seat (on bicycle)	η παιδική σέλα	i pedhikí séla
chin	το πηγούνι	to pighóoni
chips	πατάτες τηγανιτές	patátes tighanités
chocolate	η σοκολάτα	i sokoláta
choose	διαλέγω	dhialégho
christian name	το (μικρό) όνομα	to (mikró) ónoma
church	η εκκλησία	i eklisía
church service	η θεία λειτουργία	i thía litooryía
cigar	το πούρο	to póoro
cigarette paper	το τσιγαρόχαρτο	to tsigharócharto
cigarette	το τσιγάρο	to tsigháro
ciné-camera	η κινηματογραφική μηχανή	i kinimatoghrafikí michaní
circle	ο κύκλος	o kíklos
circus	το τσίρκο	to tsírko
city	η πόλη	i póli
classical concert	η κλασσική συναυλία	i klasikí sinavlía
clean (verb)	καθαρίζω	katharízo
clean	καθαρός	katharós
clear (adj.)	σαφής	safís
clearance sale	το ξεπούλημα	to xepóolima

closed off	κλειστός	*klistós*
closed	κλειστός	*klistós*
clothes peg	το μανταλάκι	*to mandaláki*
clothes	τα ρούχα	*ta róocha*
clothes hanger	η κρεμάστρα	*i kremástra*
coach	το πούλμαν	*to póolman*
coat	το παλτό	*to paltó*
cobbler	ο τσαγκάρης	*o tsangáris*
cockroach	η κατσαρίδα	*i katsarídha*
cod (dried)	ο μπακαλιάρος	*o bakalyáros*
coffee	ο καφές	*o kafés*
cold (disease)	το κρυολόγημα	*to kriolóyima*
cold	κρύος	*kríos*
cold meats	τα αλλαντικά	*ta alandiká*
collarbone	το κλειδοκόκαλο	*to klidhokókalo*
colleague	ο συνάδερφος	*o sinádherfos*
collision	η σύγκρουση	*i síngroosi*
cologne	η κολόνια	*i kolónya*
colour television	η έγχρωμη τηλεόραση	*i éngchromi tileórasi*
colour	το χρώμα	*to chróma*
coloured pencils	τα κραγιόνια	*ta krayónya*
comb	το χτένι	*to chténi*
come	έρχομαι	*érchome*
come back	ξαναέρχομαι	*xanaérchome*
compact disc	το κόμπακτ-ντισκ	*to kómpakt-disk*
compartment	το κουπέ	*to koopé*
complaint	το παράπονο	*to parápono*
complaints book	το βιβλίο παραπόνων	*to vivlío parapónon*
completely	τελείως	*telíos*
compliment	το κομπλιμέντο	*to kompliméndo*
compulsory	υποχρεωτικός	*ipochreotikós*
concert hall	η αίθουσα συναυλιών	*i éthoosa sinavlyón*
concert	η συναυλία	*i sinavlía*
concussion	η διάσειση εγκεφάλου	*i dhiásisi engkefáloo*
condom	το προφυλακτικό	*to profilaktikó*
confectioner	ο ζαχαροπλάστης	*o zacharoplástis*
congratulate	συγχαίρω	*sinchéro*
connection	η ανταπόκριση	*i andapókrisi*
constipation	η δυσκοιλιότητα	*i dhiskilyótita*
consulate	το προξενείο	*to proxenío*
consultation	η επίσκεψη	*i epískepsi*
contact lens	ο φακός επαφής	*o fakós epafís*
contact lens solution	το υγρό για φακούς επαφής	*to ighró ya fakóos epafís*
contagious	κολλητικός	*kolitikós*
contraceptive pill	το αντισυλληπτικό χάπι	*to andisiliptikó chápi*
contraceptive	το αντισυλληπτικό	*to andisiliptikó*
cook	ο μάγειρας	*o máyiras*
cook (verb)	μαγειρεύω	*mayirévo*
copper/bronze	χάλκινος	*chálkinos*
copy	το αντίγραφο	*to andíghrafo*
corkscrew	το τιρμπουσόν	*to tirbooshón*
corner	η γωνιά	*i ghonyá*
cornflower	το κορν φλάουερ	*to kornfláwer*
correct	σωστός	*sostós*
correspond	αλληλογραφώ	*aliloghrafó*
corridor	ο διάδρομος	*o dhiádhromos*

cot	το παιδικό κρεβάτι	to pedhikó kreváti
cotton wool	το βαμβάκι	o vamváki
cotton	το βαμβάκι	to vamváki
cough syrup	το σιρόπι για το βήχα	to sirópi ya to vícha
cough	ο βήχας	o víchas
counter	η θυρίδα	i thirídha
country	η χώρα	i chóra
country (dialling) code	ο αριθμός της χώρας	o arithmós tis chóras
countryside	η εξοχή	i exohí
courgette	το κολοκυθάκι	to kolokitháki
course of treatment	η θεραπεία	i therapía
cousin (female)	η ξαδέρφη	i xadhérfi
cousin (male)	ο ξάδερφος	o xádherfos
crab	ο κάβουρας	o kávooras
cream (ointment)	η κρέμα	i kréma
cream	το ανθόγαλα	to anthóghala
credit card	η πιστωτική κάρτα	i pistotikí kárta
crisps	τα τσιπς	ta tsips
cross the road	περνώ το δρόμο	to dhrómo
crossing	το πέρασμα	to pérazma
cry (verb)	κλαίω	kléo
cubic metre	το κυβικό μέτρο	to kivikó métro
cucumber	το αγγούρι	to anghóori
cuff links	τα μανικετόκουμπα	ta maniketókoomba
cup	το φλιτζάνι	to flidzáni
curly	σγουρός	zghoorós
current (water)	το ρεύμα	to révma
current (electricity)	το ρεύμα	to révma
cushion	το μαξιλαράκι	to maxilaráki
custard	η κρέμα	i kréma
customary	συνηθισμένος	sinithizménos
customs officer	ο τελώνης	o telónis
customs check	ο τελωνιακός έλεγχος	o teloniakós élenchos
customs	το τελωνείο	to telonío
cut (verb)	κόβω	kóvo
cutlery	τα μαχαιροπήρουνα	ta maheropíroona
cyclist	ο ποδηλάτης	o podhilátis

D

damage	η βλάβη	i vlávi
dance (verb)	χορεύω	chorévo
dandruff	η πιτυρίδα	i pitirídha
danger	ο κίνδυνος	o kíndhinos
dangerous	επικίνδυνος	epikíndhinos
dark	σκοτεινός	skotinós
daughter	η κόρη	i kóri
day after tomorrow	μεθαύριο	methávrio
day	η μέρα	i méra
day (24 hours)	το μερόνυχτο	to merónichto
day before yesterday	προχτές	prochtés
dead	νεκρός	nekrós
decaffeinated	χωρίς καφεΐνη	chorís kafeíni
December	ο Δεκέμβριος	o dekémvrios
deck chair	η ξαπλώστρα, η σαιζ-λόνγκ	i xaplóstra, i sezlóng
declare (customs)	δηλώνω	dhilóno
deep	βαθύς	vathís

Word list

15

117

deep-frozen	καταψυγμένος	katapsighménos
deep-sea diving	η κατάδυση σε μεγάλο βάθος	i katáthisi se meghálo váthos
defective	ελαττωματικός	elatomatikós
degrees	οι βαθμοί	i vathmí
delay (noun)	η καθυστέρηση	i kathistérisi
delicious	εξαιρετικός	exeretikós
dentist	ο οδοντογιατρός	o odhondoyatrós
dentures	η μασέλα	maséla
deodorant	το αποσμητικό	to apozmitikó
department store	ο εμπορικός οίκος	o emborikós íkos
department	το τμήμα	to tmíma
departure time	η ώρα αναχώρησης	i óra anachórisis
departure	η αναχώρηση	i anachórisi
depilatory cream	το αποτριχωτικό	to apotrichotikó
deposit	η εγγύηση	i engíisi
dessert	το επιδόρπιο	to epidhórpyo
destination	ο προορισμός	o pro-orizmós
details (personal etc.)	τα στοιχεία	ta stihía
develop (film)	εμφανίζω	emfanízo
diabetic	ο διαβητικός	o dhiavitikós
dial	παίρνω	pérno
diamond	το διαμάντι	to dhiamándi
diarrhoea	η διάρροια	i dhiária
dictionary	το λεξικό	to lexikó
diesel oil	το (λάδι)	to (ládhi) dízel
diet	η δίαιτα	i dhíeta
difficulty	η δυσκολία	i dhiskolía
dine	δειπνώ	dhipnó
dining room	η τραπεζαρία	i trapezaría
dining-car	το βαγόνι-εστιατόριο	to vaghóni-estiatório
dinner jacket	το σμόκιν	to smókin
dinner	το δείπνο	to dhípno
direction	η κατεύθυνση	i katéfthinsi
directly	κατ' ευθείαν	katefthían
dirty	βρόμικος	vrómikos
disabled	ανάπηρος	anápiros
disco	η ντίσκο	i dísko
discount	η έκπτωση	i ékptosi
dish of the day	το πιάτο της ημέρας	to pyáto tis iméras
disinfectant	το απολυμαντικό	to apolimandikó
displeased, I am	μου κακοφαίνεται	moo kakofnete
distance	η απόσταση	i apóstasi
distilled water	το διυλισμένο νερό	to dhiilizméno neró
disturb	ενοχλώ	enochló
disturbance	η διατάραξη	i dhiatáraxi
dive	βουτώ	vootó
diving	η κατάδυση	i katádhisi
diving gear	τα εξαρτήματα κατάδυσης	ta exartímata katádhisis
diving board	ο βατήρας	o vatíras
divorced	χωρισμένος	chorizménos
dizzy	ζαλισμένος	zalizménos
do night duty	διανυκτερεύω	dhianikterévo
do	κάνω	káno
doctor	ο γιατρός	o yatrós
dog	ο σκύλος	o skílos

doll	η κούκλα	o kóokla
domestic (e.g. flights)	εσωτερικός	esoterikós
door	η πόρτα	i pórta
double/for two	για δύο άτομα	ya dhío átoma
down	κάτω	káto
drachma	η δραχμή	i dhrachmí
draught, there's a	κάνει ρεύμα	káni révma
dream	ονειρεύομαι	onirévome
dress	το φόρεμα	to fórema
dressing gown	η ρόμπα	i róba
dried fruit	ξηροί καρποί	xirí karpí
drink (verb)	πίνω	píno
drink	το ποτό	to potó
drinking chocolate	το γάλα με κακάο	to ghála me kakáo
drinking water	το πόσιμο νερό	to pósimo neró
drive	οδηγώ	odhighó
driver	ο οδηγός	o odhighós
driving licence	η άδεια οδηγήσεως	i ádhya odhiyíseos
drought	η ξηρασία	i xirasía
dry clean	στεγνοκαθαρίζω	steghnokatharízo
dry cleaner's	το στεγνοκαθαριστήριο	to steghnokatharistírio
dry (verb)	στεγνώνω	steghnóno
dry	ξηρός	xirós
dry shampoo	το στεγνό σαμπουάν	to steghnó sampwán
dummy	η πιπίλα	i pipíla
during the day	την ημέρα	tin iméra
during	κατά την διάρκεια	katá ti dhiarkía

E

ear, node and throat specialist	ο ωτορινολαρυγγολόγος	o otorinolaringhológhos
ear drops	οι σταγόνες για τα αυτιά	i staghónes ya ta aftyá
ear	το αυτί	to aftí
early	νωρίς	norís
earrings	τα σκουλαρίκια	ta skoolaríkya
earth	το χώμα	to chóma
earthenware	η κεραμική	i keramikí
east	η ανατολή	i anatolí
easy	εύκολος	éfkolos
eat	τρώω	tró-o
eczema	το έκζεμα	to ékzema
eel	το χέλι	to héli
egg	το αυγό	to avghó
elastic band	το λαστιχάκι	to lasticháki
electric	ηλεκτρικός	ilektrikós
electrical connection	η ηλεκτρική σύνδεση	i ilektrikí síndhesi
embassy	η πρεσβεία	i prezvía
emergency signal	το σήμα κινδύνου	to síma kindhínoo
emergency triangle	το τρίγωνο κινδύνου	to tríghono kindhínoo
emergency exit	η έξοδος κινδύνου	i éxodhos kindhínoo
emergency number	ο αριθμός του συναγερμού	arithmós too sinayermóo
empty	άδειος	ádhyos
engaged (phone)	κατειλημμένο	katiliméno
England	η Αγγλία	i anglía
English	τα αγγλικά	ta angliká

Englishman/woman	ο Αγγλος/η Αγγλίδα	o ánglos/i anglídha
enjoy	απολαμβάνω	apolamváno
entertainment	η διασκέδαση	i dhiaskédhasi
entertainment guide (Athens only)	το Αθηνόραμα	to athinórama
entrance	η είσοδος	i ísodhos
envelope	ο φάκελος	o fákelos
environment	το περιβάλλον	to periválon
escort	η/ο συνοδός	io sinodhós
essentially	ουσιαστικά	oosiastiká
evening dress	η βραδινή ενδυμασία	i vradhiní endhimasía
evening	το βράδυ	to vrádhi
evening meal	το δείπνο	to dhípno
event	το γεγονός	to yeghonós
every time	κάθε φορά	káthe forá
everything	τα πάντα	ta pánda
everywhere	παντού	pandóo
examine	εξετάζω	exetázo
excavations	οι ανασκαφές	i anaskafés
excellent	υπέροχος	ipérochos
exchange (money)	αλλάζω	alázo
exchange	ανταλλάσσω	antaláso
excursion	η εκδρομή	i ekdhromí
exhibition	η έκθεση	i ékthesi
exit	η έξοδος	i éxodhos
expenses	τα έξοδα	ta éxodha
expensive	ακριβός	akrivós
explain	εξηγώ	exighó
express train	η ταχεία	i tahía
external	εξωτερικός	exoterikós
eye specialist	ο οφθαλμίιατρος	o ofthalmíatros
eye	το μάτι	to máti
eyedrops	οι σταγόνες για τα μάτια	i staghónes ya ta mátya
eyeliner	το μολύβι για τα μάτια	to molívi ya ta mátya

F

face	το πρόσωπο	to prósopo
factory	το εργοστάσιο	to erghostásyo
fall	πέφτω	péfto
family	η οικογένεια	i ikoyénya
famous	ξακουστός	xakoostós
far away	μακριά	makriá
farm	το αγρόκτημα	to aghróktima
farmer	ο γεωργός	o yeorghós
fashion	η μόδα	i módha
father	ο πατέρας	o patéras
fax (verb)	στέλνω ένα φαξ	stélno éna fax
February	ο Φεβρουάριος	o fevrooários
feel like	έχω διάθεση	écho dhiáthesi
feel like	αισθάνομαι	esthánome
ferry	το φέρρυ-μπωτ	to féribot
festival	η γιορτή	i yortí
fever	ο πυρετός	o piretós
fill (tooth)	σφραγίζω	sfrayízo

Word list

15

fill/top up	γεμίζω	yemízo
fill out	συμπληρώνω	simpliróno
filling	το σφράγισμα	to sfráyizma
film	η ταινία	i tenía
film (camera)	το φιλμ	to film
filter	το φίλτρο	to fíltro
find	βρίσκω	vrísko
fine	η κλήση	i klísi
finger	το δάχτυλο	to dháchtilo
fingernail	το νύχι	to níhi
fire escape	η σκάλα πυρκαγιάς	i skála pirkayás
fire	η φωτιά	i fotyá
fire (accidental)	η πυρκαγιά	i pirkayá
fire extinguisher	ο πυροσβεστήρας	o pirosvestíras
fire brigade	η πυροσβεστική υπηρεσία	i pirosvestikí ipiresía
first aid	οι πρώτες βοήθειες	i prótes voíthyes
first class	η πρώτη θέση	i próti thési
first	πρώτος	prótos
fish (verb)	ψαρεύω	psarévo
fish	το ψάρι	to psári
fishing rod	το αγκίστρι	to angístri
fitness centre	το γυμναστήριο	to yimnastírio
fitting room	το δοκιμαστήριο	to dhokimastíryo
fix	φτιάχνω	ftyáchno
flag	η σημαία	i siméa
flash bulb	η λάμπα φλας	i lámpa flash
flash gun	το φλας	to flash
flash cubes	οι λάμπες φλας	i lámpes flash
flea market	το παλιατζίδικο	to paliatzídhiko
flight	η πτήση	i ptísi
flight number	ο αριθμός της πτήσης	o arithmós tis ptísis
flood	η πλημμύρα	i plimíra
floor	ο όροφος	o órofos
flour	το αλεύρι	to alévri
flu	η γρίπη	i ghrípi
fly	η μύγα	i mígha
fly (verb)	πετώ	petó
flyover	η οδογέφυρα	i odhoyéfira
foggy, it is	έχει ομίχλη	éhi omíchli
folding caravan	το λυόμενο τροχόσπιτο	to liómeno trochóspito
folkloristic	λαογραφικός	laoghrafikós
follow	ακολουθώ	akoloothó
food poisoning	η τροφική δηλητηρίαση	i trofikí dhilitiríasi
food	το φαγητό	to fayitó
food	τα τρόφιμα	ta trófima
foot	το πόδι	to pódhi
football	το ποδόσφαιρο	to podhósfero
football match	ο ποδοσφαιρικός αγώνας	o podhosferikós aghónas
for hire	ενοικιάζεται	nikyázete
forbidden, it is	απαγορεύεται	apaghorévete
forehead	το μέτωπο	to métopo
foreign	εξωτερικός	exoterikós
forget	ξεχνάω	xechnáo
fork	το πηρούνι	to piróoni
form	το έντυπο	to éndipo

fort	το κάστρο	to kástro
fountain	το συντριβάνι	to sindriváni
frame	ο σκελετός	o skeletós
free	ελεύθερος	eléftheros
free time	η ελεύθερη ώρα	i eléftheri óra
freeze	παγώνω	paghóno
French	τα γαλλικά	ta ghaliká
French bread	το ψωμί μπαστούνι	to psomí bastóoni
fresh	φρέσκος	fréskos
Friday	η Παρασκευή	i paraskeví
fried	τηγανητός	tighanitós
fried egg	το αυγό μάτι	to avghó máti
friend	ο φίλος	o fílos
friendly	ευγενικός	evyenikós
fringe	η φράντζα	i frándza
fritter	η τηγανίτα	i tighaníta
front, at the	μπροστά	brostá
frozen	καταψυγμένος	katapsighménos
fruit	το φρούτο	to fróoto
fruit juice	ο χυμός	o chimós
frying pan	το τηγάνι	to tigháni
full	γεμάτος	yemátos

G

gallery (theatre)	ο εξώστης	o exóstis
game	το παιχνίδι	to pechnídhi
garage	το γκαράζ	to garáz
garbage bag	η σακούλα σκουπιδιών	i sakóola skoopidhyón
garden	ο κήπος	o kípos
gauze	η γάζα	i gháza
gear	η ταχύτητα	i tahítita
gel	το τζελ	to dzel
gentleman	ο κύριος	o kírios
German	τα γερμανικά	ta yermaniká
get off/out	κατεβαίνω	katevéno
get lost	χάνω το δρόμο	cháno to dhrómo
gift	το δώρο	to dhóro
girl	το κορίτσι	to korítsi
girl friend	η φίλη	i fíli
giro cheque	η ταχυδρομική επιταγή	i tahidhromikí epitayí
giro card	η ταχυδρομική κάρτα	i tahidhromikí kárta
glass	το ποτήρι	to potíri
glasses (sun-, reading-)	τα γυαλιά	ta yalyá
gliding	η ανεμοπορία	i anemaporía
glove	το γάντι	to ghándi
glue	η κόλλα	i kóla
go out	βγαίνω έξω	vyéno éxo
go back	γυρίζω	yirízo
go	πηγαίνω	piyéno
goat's cheese	το κατσικίσιο τυρί	to katsikísyo tirí
gold	το χρυσάφι	to chrisáfi
gold-plated	επίχρυσος	epíchrisos
golf course	το γήπεδο του γκολφ	to yípedho too golf
golf	το γκολφ	to golf
good afternoon	καλημέρα	kaliméra
good night	καληνύχτα	kaliníchta
good day	καλημέρα	kaliméra

good luck	η ευτυχία	i eftihía
good morning	καλημέρα	kaliméra
good evening	καλησπέρα	kalispéra
goodbye	γειά σας, γειά σου	yásas, yásoo
goodbye (farewell)	ο αποχαιρετισμός	o apoheretizmós
gram	το γραμμάριο	to ghramário
grandchild	το εγγόνι	to engóni
grandfather	ο παππούς	o papóos
grandmother	η γιαγιά	i yayá
grape juice	ο χυμός σταφυλιών	o chimós stafilyón
grapefruit	η φράπα	i frápa
grapes	τα σταφύλια	ta stafílya
gratis	δωρεάν	dhoreán
grave	ο τάφος	o táfos
grease	τα λίπη	ta lípi
green card	η πράσινη κάρτα	i prásini kárta
green	πράσινος	prásinos
greet	χαιρετίζω	heretízo
greetings	τα χαιρετίσματα	ta heretízmata
grey	γκρίζος	grízos
grill (verb)	ψήνω στα κάρβουνα	psíno sta kárvoona
grilled	ψητός	psitós
grocer	ο μπακάλης	o bakális
ground	το χώμα	to chóma
group	το γκρουπ	to groop
guest house	η πανσιόν	i pansyón
guide (person)	ο ξεναγός	o xenaghós
guidebook	ο οδηγός	o odhighós
guided tour	η ξενάγηση	i xenáyisi
guilt	η ενοχή	i enohí
gynaecologist	ο γυναικολόγος	o yinekológhos

H

hair cream	το βερνίκι για τα μαλλιά	to verníki ya ta malyá
hair	τα μαλλιά	ta malyá
hairdresser	ο κομμωτής	o komotís
hairpins	οι καρφίτσες	i karfítses
half kilo	το μισό κιλό	to misó kiló
half	μισό	misó
half-full	μισογεμάτος	misoyemátos
ham	το ζαμπόν	to zambón
hammer	το σφυρί	to sfirí
hand brake	το χειρόφρενο	to hirófreno
hand	το χέρι	to héri
handbag	η τσάντα	i tsánda
handmade	χειροποίητος	hiroplítos
handicraft	η χειροτεχνία	i hirotechnía
handkerchief	το μαντήλι	to mandíli
handsome	ωραίος	oréos
happy	χαρούμενος	charóomenos
harbour	το λιμάνι	to limáni
hard	σκληρός	sklirós
hat	το καπέλο	to kapélo
hayfever	ο αλλεργικός κατάρρους	o aleryikós katároos
hazelnut	το φουντούκι	to foondóoki

head	το κεφάλι	to kefáli
headache	ο πονοκέφαλος	o ponokéfalos
health	η υγεία	i iyía
heart patient	ο καρδιακός	o kardhiakós
heart	η καρδιά	i kardhyá
heater	το καλοριφέρ	to kalorifér
heavy	βαρύς	varís
hedge	ο φράχτης	o fráchtis
heel (of shoe)	το τακούνι	to takóoni
hello	γειά σας, γειά σου	yásas, yásoo
helmet	το κράνος	to krános
help	η βοήθεια	i voíthya
help (verb)	βοηθώ	voithó
herb tea	το τσάι του βουνού	to tsái too voonóo
herbs	τα μπαχαρικά	ta bacharciká
here	εδώ	edhó
herring (smoked)	η ρέγγα	rénga
high tide	η παλίρροια	i palíria
high chair	η παιδική καρέκλα	i pedhikí karékla
high	ψηλός	psilós
hiking	η πεζοπορία	i pezoporía
hip	ο γοφός	o ghofós
hire	νοικιάζω	nikyázo
hitch-hiking	το ωτοστόπ	to otostóp
hobby	το χόμπυ	to chóbi
hold-up	η επίθεση	i epíthesi
holiday cottage	το εξοχικό σπιτάκι	to exohikó spitáki
holiday (public)	η γιορτή	i yortí
holidays	οι διακοπές	i dhiakopés
homesickness	η νοσταλγία	i nostalyía
honest	τίμιος	tímyos
honey	το μέλι	to méli
horizontal	οριζόντιος	orizóndios
horrible	απαίσιος	apésios
horse	το άλογο	to álogho
hospital	το νοσοκομείο	to nosokomío
hospitality	η φιλοξενία	i filoxenía
hot	ζεστός	zestós
hot (spicy)	πικάντικος	pikándikos
hot spring	η θερμική πηγή	i thermikí piyí
hot-water bottle	η θερμοφόρα	i thermofóra
hotel	το ξενοδοχείο	to xenodhohío
hour	η ώρα	i óra
house	το σπίτι	to spíti
household items	τα οικιακά αντικείμενα	ta ikyaká andikímena
housewife	η νοικοκυρά	i nikokirá
how	πώς;	pos?
how far?	πόσο μακριά;	póso makriá?
how much?	πόσο;	póso?
how long?	πόσο καιρό;	póso kyeró?
hundred grams	εκατό γραμμάρια	ekató ghramárya
hunger	η πείνα	i pína
hurricane	ο τυφώνας	o tifónas
hurry (be in a)	βιάζομαι	vyázome
husband	ο σύζυγος	o sízighos
hut	η καλύβα	i kalíva
hyperventilation	η υπεροξυγόνωση	i iperoxighónosi

I

ice	ο πάγος	o pághos
ice-cream	το παγωτό	to paghotó
ice-cubes	τα παγάκια	ta paghákya
idea	η ιδέα	i idhéa
identification	η ταυτότητα	i taftótita
identify	αναγνωρίζω	anaghnorízo
ignition key	το κλειδί επαφής	to klidhí epafís
illness	η αρρώστια	i aróstia
illustrated book	το εικονογραφημένο βιβλίο	to ikonoghrafiméno vivlío
imagine	φαντάζομαι	fandázome
immediately	αμέσως	amésos
import duty	τα εισαγωγικά τέλη	ta isaghoyiká téli
impossible	αδύνατος	adhínatos
in front of	μπροστά σε	brostá se
in	σε	se
in front	μπροστά	brostá
in safe-keeping	σε φύλαξη	se fílaxi
in the evening/at night	το βράδυ	to vrádhi
included (it is)	συμπεριλαμβάνεται	simperilamvánete
indicate	δείχνω	dhíchno
indicator	το φλας	to flash
indigestion	η δυσπεψία	i dhispepsía
inflammation	η φλεγμονή	i fleghmoní
information office	το γραφείο πληροφοριών	to ghrafío pliroforyón
information	οι πληροφορίες	i plirofories
information (piece of)	η πληροφορία	i plirofória
injection	η ένεση	i énesi
injured	λαβωμένος	lavoménos
inner tube	το εσωτερικό λάστιχο	to esoterikó lásticho
innocent	αθώος	athóos
insect	το έντομο	to éndomo
insect repellent	λάδι για τα κουνούπια	ládhi ya ta koonóopya
insect bite	το τσίμπημα εντόμου	to tsímbima endómoo
inside	μέσα	mésa
insole	η εσωτερική σόλα	i esoterikí sóla
instructions for use	οι οδηγίες χρήσεως	i odhiyíes chríseos
insurance	η ασφάλεια	i asfálya
internal	εσωτερικός	esoterikós
international	διεθνής	dhiethnís
interpreter	ο διερμηνέας	o dhierminéas
intersection	η διασταύρωση	i dhiastávrosi
interval	το διάλειμμα	to dhiálima
introduce	γνωρίζω	ghnorízo
introduce myself	συστήνομαι	sistínome
invite	προσακλώ	proskaló
iodine	το ιώδιο	to iódhio
Ireland	η Ιρλανδία	i irlandhía
Irishman	ο Ιρλανδός/η Ιρλανδέζα	o irlandhós/i irlandhéza
iron	το σίδερο	to sídhero
iron (verb)	σιδερώνω	sidheróno
ironing board	η σανίδα σιδερώματος	i sanídha sidherómatos
island	το νησί	to nisí
Italian	τα ιταλικά	ta italiká

Word list

15

itch	η φαγούρα	i faghóora
item of clothing	το ρούχο	to róocho
itinerary	το δρομολόγιο	to dhromolóyo

J

jack	ο γρύλλος	o ghrílos
jacket	η ζακέτα	i zakéta
jam	η μαρμελάδα	i marmeládha
January	ο Ιανουάριος	o yanooários
jaw	το σαγόνι	to saghóni
jellyfish	η μέδουσα	i médhoosa
jeweller	ο χρυσοχόος	o chrisochóos
jewellery	τα κοσμήματα	ta kozmímata
jog (running)	το τρέξιμο	to tréximo
joke	το αστείο	to astío
juice	ο χυμός	o himós
July	ο Ιούλιος	o yóolios
jump leads	το καλώδιο εκκίνησης	to kalódhio ekkínisis
jumper	το πουλόβερ	o poolóver
June	ο Ιούνιος	o yóonios
junk shop	το παλιατζίδικο	to paliadzídhiko

K

kettle	ο βραστήρας	o vrastíras
key	το κλειδί	to klidhí
kilo	το κιλό	to kiló
kilometer	το χιλιόμετρο	to hilyómetro
king	ο βασιλιάς	o vasilyás
kiosk	το περίπτερο	to períptero
kiss	το φιλί	to filí
kiss (verb)	φιλώ	filó
kitchen	η κουζίνα	i koozína
knee	το γόνατο	to ghónato
knife	το μαχαίρι	to machéri
knit	πλέκω	pléko
know (person)	γνωρίζω	ghnorízo
know	ξέρω	xéro

L

lace	η δαντέλα	i dhantéla
ladies' toilet	η τουαλέτα γυναικών	i twaléta yinekón
lady	η κυρία	i kiría
lake	η λίμνη	i límni
lamb chop	το παϊδάκι	to paidháki
lamp	η λάμπα	i lámpa
land (verb)	προσγειώνομαι	prosyiónome
lane (on road)	η λωρίδα	i lorídha
language	η γλώσσα	i ghlóssa
lard	το λαρδί	to lardhí
large	μεγάλος	meghálos
last	τελευταίος	teleftéos
last night	χθες τη νύχτα	chthes ti níchta
late	αργά	arghá
latest, at the	το αργότερο	to arghótero
laugh	γελάω	yeláo
launderette	το πλυντήριο	to plindírio
lavatory	η τουαλέτα	i twaléta

law (studies)	τα νομικά	ta nomiká
lawyer	ο δικηγόρος	o dhikighóros
laxative	το καθαρτικό	to kathartikó
leaking	τρυπημένος	tripiménos
leather	το δέρμα	to dhérma
leather goods	τα δερμάτινα είδη	ta dhermátina ídhi
leave (verb)	φεύγω	févgho
leek	το πράσο	to práso
left luggage locker	η θυρίδα αποσκευών	i thirídha aposkevón
left (adj.)	αριστερός	aristerós
left (on/to the)	αριστερά	aristerá
left luggage office	ο χώρος αποσκευών	o chóros aposkevón
leg	το πόδι	to pódhi
lemon	το λεμόνι	to lemóni
lemonade	η λεμονάδα	i lemonádha
lens	ο φακός	o fakós
lentils	οι φακές	i fakés
less	λιγότερο	lighótero
lesson	το μάθημα	to máthima
letter	το γράμμα	to ghrámma
lettuce	το μαρούλι	to maróoli
level crossing	η διάβαση	i dhiávasi
library	η βιβλιοθήκη	i vivliothíki
lie down	ξαπλώνομαι	xaplónome
lie	λέω ψέματα	léo psémata
lifeguard	ο ακτοφύλακας	o aktofílakas
lift	το ασανσέρ/ ο ανελκυστήρας	to asansér/o anelkistíras
light (colour)	ανοιχτός	anichtós
light (weight)	ελαφρός	elafrós
light	το φως	o fos
lighter	ο αναπτήρας	o anaptíras
lighthouse	ο φάρος	o fáros
lightning	ο κεραυνός	o keravnós
like, I	μ' αρέσει	marési
line	η γραμμή	i ghramí
linen	το λινό	to linó
lipstick	το κραγιόν	to krayón
listen	ακούω	akóo-o
literature	η λογοτεχνία	i loghotechnía
litre	το λίτρο	to lítro
little	λίγος	líghos
live	μένω	méno
live together	συγκατοικώ	singkatikó
lively	ζωηρός	zoirós
lobster	ο αστακός	o astakós
local	τοπικός	topikós
local (dialling) code	ο κωδικός της πόλης	o kodhikós tis pólis
lock	η κλειδαριά	i klidharyá
long (tall)	μακρύς	makrís
long (of time)	πολύς	polís
look	κοιτάζω	kitázo
lorry	το καμιόνι	to kamyóni
lose	χάνω	cháno
loss	ο χαμός, η απώλεια	o chamós, i apólya
lost property	τα ευρεθέντα αντικείμενα	ta evrethénda andikímena

lost	χαμένος	_chaménos_
lotion	η λοσιόν	_i losión_
loud	δυνατά	_dhinatá_
love with, be in	είμαι ερωτευμένος με	_íme erotevménos me_
love (verb)	αγαπώ	_aghapó_
love	η αγάπη	_i aghápi_
low tide	η άμπωτη	_i ámboti_
low	χαμηλός	_chamilós_
luggage	οι αποσκευές	_i aposkevés_
luggage locker	η θυρίδα αποσκευών	_i thirídha aposkevón_
lunch	το γεύμα	_to yévma_
lungs	οι πνεύμονες	_i pnévmones_

M

machine	η μηχανή	_i michaní_
magazine	το περιοδικό	_to periodhikó_
mail	το ταχυδρομείο	_to tahidhromío_
main road	ο μεγάλος δρόμος	_o meghálos dhrómos_
main post-office	το κεντρικό ταχυδρομείο	_to kendrikó tahidhromío_
make an appointment/ a date	δίνω ραντεβού	_dhíno randevóo_
make love	κάνω έρωτα	_káno érota_
man	ο άντρας	_o ándras_
manager	ο διαχειριστής	_o dhiahiristís_
mandarin (orange)	το μανταρίνι	_to mandaríni_
manicure	το μανικιούρ	_to manikyóor_
map	ο χάρτης	_o chártis_
marble	το μάρμαρο	_to mármaro_
March	ο Μάρτιος	_o mártis_
margarine	η μαργαρίνη	_i margharíni_
marina	η μαρίνα	_i marína_
market	η αγορά	_i aghorá_
marriage	ο γάμος	_o ghámos_
married	παντρεμένος	_pandreménos_
married, get	παντρεύομαι	_pandrévome_
massage	το μασάζ	_to masáz_
matt (photographs)	ματ	_mat_
match	ο αγώνας	_o aghónas_
matches	τα σπίρτα	_ta spírta_
May	Ο Μάιος	_o máios_
maybe	ίσως	_ísos_
mayonnaise	η μαγιονέζα	_i mayonéza_
mayor	ο δήμαρχος	_o dhímarchos_
meal	το γεύμα	_to yévma_
mean	σημαίνω	_siméno_
means	το μέσο	_to méso_
meat	το κρέας	_to kréas_
medication	το φάρμακο	_to fármako_
medicine (liquid)	το σιρόπι	_to sirópi_
medicine	το φάρμακο	_to fármako_
melon	το πεπόνι	_to pepóni_
membership	η ιδιότητα του μέλους	_i idhiótita too méloos_
menstruate	έχω περίοδο	_écho período_
menstruation	η περίοδος	_i períodhos_
menu of the day	το μενού της ημέρας	_to menóo tis iméras_
menu	το μενού, ο κατάλογος	_to menóo o katáloghos_

15

message	η παραγγελία	i parangelía
metal	το μέταλλο	to métalo
meter	ο μετρητής	o metritís
metre	το μέτρο	to métro
middle, in the	στη μέση	sti mési
migraine	η ημικρανία	i imikranía
mild (tobacco)	ελαφρός	elafrós
milk	το γάλα	to ghála
milk products	τα προϊόντα γάλακτος	ta proiónda ghálaktos
milk for coffee	το γάλα για τον καφέ	to ghála ya tongafé
millimetre	το χιλιοστόμετρο	to hilyostómetro
milometer	το κοντέρ	o kontér
mince	ο κιμάς	o kimás
mineral water	το μεταλλικό νερό	to metalikó neró
minute	το λεπτό	to leptó
mirror	ο καθρέφτης	o kathréftis
miss (I)	μου λείπει	moo lípi
missing (is)	λείπει	lípi
missing (person)	χαμένος	chaménos
mist	η ομίχλη	i omíchli
mistake	το λάθος	to láthos
mistaken, be	κάνω λάθος	káno láthos
Mister	ο κύριος	o kírios
misunderstanding	η παρεξήγηση	i parexíyisi
mocha	η μόκα	i móka
modern art	η σύγχρονη τέχνη	i singchroni téchni
molar	ο τραπεζίτης	o trapezítis
moment	η στιγμή	i stighmí
monastery	το μοναστήρι	to monastíri
Monday	η Δευτέρα	i deftéra
money	τα λεφτά	ta leftá
month	ο μήνας	o mínas
moped	το μηχανάκι	to michanáki
morning (in the)	το πρωί	to proí
morning-after-pill	το μόρνιγκ-άφτερ-χάπι	to mórning-áfter-chápi
mosque	το τζαμί	to dzamí
mosquito	το κουνούπι	to koonóopi
motel	το μοτέλ	to motél
mother	η μητέρα	i mitéra
motorboat	η βενζινάκατος	i venzinákatos
motorcycle	η μοτοσικλέτα	i motosikléta
motorway	η εθνική οδός	i ethnikí odhós
mountain boots	τα παπούτσια ορειβασίας	ta papóotsia orivasías
mountain hut	το ορειβατικό καταφύγιο	to orivatikó katafíyo
mountain	το βουνό	to voonó
mountaineering	η ορειβασία	i orivasía
mouse	το ποντίκι	to pondíki
mouth	το στόμα	to stóma
move back	κάνω πίσω	káno píso
Mrs	η κυρία	i kiría
much/many	πολύς	polís
multistory carpark	το σκεπασμένο πάρκιγκ	to skepazméno párking
muscle spasm	ο σπασμός	o spazmós
muscle	ο μυς	o mis

Word list 15

museum	το μουσείο	to moosío
mushrooms	τα μανιτάρια	ta manitárya
music	η μουσική	i moosikí
musical (show)	η μουσική κωμωδία	i moosikí komodhía
mussels	τα μύδια	ta mídhya
mustard	η μουστάρδα	i moostárdha
my name is	λέγομαι/με λένε	léghome/me léne

N

nail varnish remover	το ασετόν	to asetón
nail varnish	το βερνίκι νυχιών	to verníki nihyón
nail scissors	το ψαλιδάκι για τα νύχια	to psalidháki yia ta níhya
nail	το καρφί	to karfí
nail file	η λίμα για τα νύχια	i líma ya ta níhya
naked	γυμνός	yimnós
napkin	η πετσέτα	i petséta
nappy	η πάνα	i pána
National Health Office	το ταμείο ασθενείας	to tamío asthenías
nationality	η υπηκοότητα	i ipikoótita
naturally	φυσικά	fisiká
nature	η φύση	i físi
nauseous, I feel	ανακατεύεται το στομάχι μου	anakatévete to stomáchi moo
near	κοντά	kondá
near to	κοντά σε	kondá se
necessary	αναγκαίος	anangéos
neck	ο σβέρκος	o zvérkos
nectarine	το νεκταρίνι	to nektaríni
needle	το βελόνι	to velóni
negative	το αρνητικό	to arnitikó
neighbours	οι γείτονες	i yítones
nephew	ο ανιψιός	o anipsyós
never	ποτέ	poté
new	καινούριος	kenóorios
news	τα νέα	ta néa
newspaper	η εφημερίδα	i efimerídha
next	επόμενος	epómenos
next to	δίπλα σε	dhípla se
nice-looking	ωραίος	oréos
nice (people, things and events)	καλός	kalós
niece	η ανιψιά	i anipsyá
night life	η νυχτερινή ζωή	i nichteriní zoí
night	το βράδυ	to vrádhi
night	η νύχτα	i níchta
nightclub	το νυχτερινό κέντρο	to nichterinó kéndro
no	όχι	óhi
no overtaking	απαγορεύεται η προσπέραση	apaghorévete i prospérasi
no one	κανένας	kanénas
noise	ο θόρυβος	o thórivos
non-stop	χωρίς σταθμούς	chorís stathmóos
nonsense	οι σαχλαμάρες	i sachlamáres
normal	κανονικός	kanonikós
north	ο βοριάς	o voryás

nose	η μύτη	i míti
nose-drops	οι σταγόνες για τη μύτη	i staghónes ya ti míti
nosebleed	η ρινορραγία	i rinorayía
notepaper	το χαρτί της αλληλογραφίας	to chartí aliloghrafías
nothing	τίποτα	típota
November	ο Νοέμβριος	o noémvrios
nowhere	πουθενά	poothená
nude	γυμνός	yimnós
nudism	ο γυμνισμός	o yimnizmós
nudist beach	η πλαζ για γυμνιστές	i plaz ya yimnistés
number plate	ο αριθμός κυκλοφορίας	o arithmós kikloforías
number	ο αριθμός	o arithmós
nurse	η νοσοκόμα	i nosokóma
nutmeg	το μοσχοκάρυδο	to moschokáridho

O

object	το αντικείμενο	to andikímeno
occupied/taken	κατειλημμένος	katiliménos
October	ο Οκτώβριος	o októvrios
off (of meat)	χαλασμένος	chalazménos
off-licence	η κάβα	i káva
offer	προσφέρω	prosféro
office	το γραφείο	to ghrafío
oil	το λάδι	to ládhi
oil level	η στάθμη του λαδιού	i státhmi too ladhyóo
ointment for burns	η αλοιφή για εγκαύματα	i alifí ya engkávmata
ointment	η αλοιφή	i alifí
OK	εντάξει	endáxi
old	μεγάλος	meghálos
olive oil	το ελαιόλαδο	eleóladho
olives	οι ελιές	i elyés
omelette	η ομελέτα	i omeléta
on	πάνω σε	páno se
onboard ship	στο πλοίο	sto plío
once	μια φορά	mya forá
one-way traffic	μονόδρομος	monódhromos
onion	το κρεμμύδι	to kremídhi
open	ανοιχτός	anichtós
open (verb)	ανοίγω	anígho
opera	η όπερα	i ópera
operate	εγχειρίζω	engchirízo
operator (telephone)	η τηλεφωνήτρια	i tilefonítria
operetta	η οπερέτα	i operéta
opposite	απέναντι	apénandi
opposite to	αντίκρυ σε	andíkri se
optician	ο οπτικός	o optikós
orange	το πορτοκάλι	to portokáli
orange juice	ο χυμός πορτοκαλιού	o himós portokalyóo
orange (coloured)	πορτοκαλής	portokalís
order (noun, e.g. a meal)	η παραγγελία	i parangelía
order (verb, e.g. a meal)	παραγγέλνω	parangélno
others	άλλοι	áli

Word list

15

out of order	χαλασμένος	*chalazménos*
outside	έξω	*éxo*
overnight duty	η διανυκτέρευση	*i dhianiktérefsi*
overtake	προσπερνάω	*prospernáo*
oysters	τα στρείδια	*ta strídhya*

P

packed lunch	το πακέτο του μεσημεριανού φαγητού	*to pakéto too mesimeryanóo fayitóo*
page	η σελίδα	*i selídha*
pain	ο πόνος	*o pónos*
pain-killer	το παυσίπονο	*to pafsípono*
paint	η μπογιά	*i boyá*
painting (art of)	η ζωγραφική	*i zoghrafikí*
painting (object)	ο πίνακας	*o pínakas*
palace	το παλάτι	*to paláti*
pan	η κατσαρόλα	*i katsaróla*
pane of glass	το τζάμι	*to dzámi*
panty liner	η μικρή πετσέτα υγείας	*i mikrí petséta iyías*
paper	το χαρτί	*to chartí*
paraffin oil	το πετρέλαιο	*to petréleo*
parasol	η ομπρέλα	*i ombréla*
parcel	το δέμα	*to dhéma*
pardon	συγγνώμη	*signómi*
parents	οι γονείς	*i ghonís*
park (verb)	παρκάρω	*parkáro*
park	το πάρκο	*to párko*
parliament (building)	η βουλή	*i voolí*
parsley	ο μαϊντανός	*o maidanós*
partner	ο/η σύζυγος	*o/i sízighos*
party	το πάρτυ	*to párti*
passable (road or stream)	βατός	*vatós*
passenger	ο επιβάτης	*o epivátis*
passport photograph	η φωτογραφία διαβατηρίου	*i fotoghrafía dhiavatiríoo*
passport	διαβατήριο	*to dhiavatíryo*
patient	ο ασθενής	*o asthenís*
pavement	το πεζοδρόμιο	*to pezodhrómio*
pay the bill	πληρώνω	*pliróno*
pay (verb)	πληρώνω	*pliróno*
pea	ο αρακάς	*o arakás*
peach	το ροδάκινο	*to rodhákino*
peanuts	τα φιστίκια	*ta fistíkya*
pear	το αχλάδι	*to achládhi*
pedestrian crossing	η διάβαση πεζών	*i dhiávasi pezón*
pedicure	το πεντικιούρ	*to pedikyóor*
pen	το στυλό	*to stiló*
pencil	το μολύβι	*to molívi*
penis	το πέος	*to péos*
pension	η σύνταξη	*i síndaxi*
pepper	το πιπέρι	*to pipéri*
pepper (vegetable)	η πιπεριά	*i piperyá*
performance	η παράσταση	*i parástasi*
perfume	το άρωμα	*to ároma*
perm (verb)	κάνω περμανάντ	*káno permanánt*
permanent wave	η περμανάντ	*i permanánt*
permit	η άδεια	*i ádhya*

person	το άτομο	to átomo
personal	προσωπικός	prosopikós
petrol	η βενζίνη	i venzíni
petrol (high-octane)	η σούπερ	i sóoper
petrol station	το βενζινάδικο	venzinádhiko
pets	τα κατοικίδια ζώα	ta kaitkídhia zóa
phone number	ο αριθμός	o arithmós
phone (verb)	τηλεφωνώ	tilefonó
phone book	ο τηλεφωνικός κατάλογος	o tilefonikós katáloghos
phone	το τηλέφωνο	to tiléfono
phone box	ο τηλεφωνικός θάλαμος	o tilefonikós thálamos
photocopier	το φωτοτυπικό μηχάνημα	to fototipikó michánima
photocopy (verb)	κάνω φωτοαντίγραφο	káno photandígrafo
photocopy	το φωτοαντίγραφο	to photandígrafo
photograph	η φωτογραφία	i fotghrafía
pick up	παίρνω	pérno
picnic	το πικνίκ	to pikník
pier	η προκυμαία	i prokiméa
pigeon	το περιστέρι	to peristéri
pill	το χάπι	to chápi
pillow	το μαξιλάρι	to maxilári
pillow-case	η μαξιλαροθήκη	i maxilarothíki
pin	η καρφίτσα	i karfítsa
pineapple	ο ανανάς	o ananás
pipe	η πίπα	i pípa
pipe tobacco	ο καπνός για την πίπα	o kapnós ya timbípa
pity	κρίμα	kríma
place of entertainment	το κέντρο	to kéndro
place	ο τόπος	o tópos
place of interest	το αξιοθέατο	to axiothéato
plan	το σχέδιο	to schédhyo
plant	το φυτό	to fitó
plastic bag	η σακούλα	i sakóola
plastic	πλαστικός	plastikós
plate	το πιάτο	to pyáto
platform	η πλατφόρμα, η γραμμή	i platfórma, i ghramí
play	το θεατρικό έργο	to theatrikó érgho
play (verb)	παίζω	pézo
playground	η παιδική χαρά	i pedhikí chará
playing cards	τα χαρτιά	ta chartyá
pleasant	ευχάριστος	efcháristos
please	παρακαλώ	parakaló
pleasure	η απόλαυση	i apólafsi
pleasure (it's a)	χαίρω πολύ	héro polí
pleasure, with	ευχαρίστως	efcháristos
plum	το δαμάσκηνο	to dhamáskino
pocket knife	ο σουγιάς	o sooyás
point	δείχνω	dhíchno
poison	το δηλητήριο	to dhilitírio
police court	το αυτόφωρο	to aftóforo
police	η αστυνομία	i astinomía
police station	το αστυνομικό τμήμα	to astinomikó tmíma
policeman	ο αστυνομικός	o astinomikós

pond	η λιμνούλα	i limnóola
pony	το πόνυ	to póni
pop concert	η συναυλία ποπ	i sinavlía pop
population	ο πληθυσμός	o plithizmós
pork	το χοιρινό κρέας	to hirinó kréas
port	το λιμάνι	to limáni
porter (doorman)	ο θυρωρός	o thirorós
porter	ο αχθοφόρος	o achthofóros
portion	η μερίδα	i merídha
post office	το ταχυδρομείο	to tahidhromío
post code	ο ταχυδρομικός κώδικας	o tahidhromikós kódhikas
post-box	το γραμματοκιβώτιο	to ghramatokivótyo
post-card	η καρτ-ποστάλ	i kartpostál
postal charges	τα ταχυδρομικά τέλη	ta tahidhromiká téli
postman	ο ταχυδρόμος	o tahidhrómos
potato	η πατάτα	i patáta

R

recovery service	ΕΛΠΑ	i elpá
refrigerator	το ψυγείο	to psiyío
region	η περιοχή	i periohí
registered	συστημένος	sistiménos
registration number	ο αριθμός κυκλοφορίας	o arithmós kikloforías
reliable	αξιόπιστος	axiópistos
religion	η θρησκεία	i thriskía
religion	η πίστη	i písti
rent out	νοικιάζω	nikyázo
repair (verb)	επιδιορθώνω	epidhiorthóno
repairs	η επιδιόρθωση	i epidhiórthosi
repeat	επαναλαμβάνω	epanalamváno
responsible	υπεύθυνος	ipéfthinos
rest	ξεκουράζομαι	xekoorázome
restaurant	το εστιατόριο	to estiatório
retired	συνταξιούχος	sintaxióochos
return (ticket)	μετ' επιστροφής	metepistrofís
reverse	κάνω όπισθεν	káno ópisthen
rheumatism	ο ρευματισμός	o revmatizmós
rice	το ρύζι	to rízi
riding school	η σχολή ιππασίας	i scholí ipasías
riding (horseback)	η ιππασία	i ipasía
right of way	η προτεραιότητα	i protereótita
right	δεξιά	dhexyá
right, on the	δεξιά	dhexyá
ripe	ώριμος	órimos
river	το ποτάμι	to potámi
road suitable for cars	ο αυτοκινητόδρομος	o aftokinitódhromos
roasted	ψημένος	psiménos
rock	ο βράχος	o vráchos
roof (flat)	η ταράτσα	i tarátsa
roof-rack	η σχάρα αυτοκινήτου	i schára aftokinítoo
room service	η εξυπηρέτηση δωματίου	i exipirétisi dhomatíoo
room number	ο αριθμός δωματίου	o arithmós dhomatíoo
room	το δωμάτιο	to dhomátyo
rope	το σκοινί	to skiní
rosé wine	κρασί ροζέ	krasí rozé

roundabout	η ροτόντα	*i rotónda*
route	η πορεία	*i poría*
rowing boat	η βάρκα	*i várka*
rubber	το λάστιχο	*to lásticho*
rucksack	το σακίδιο	*to sakídhyo*
rude	αγενής	*ayenís*
ruins	τα ερείπια	*ta erípya*
run into	συναντώ	*sinandó*

S

sad	θλιμμένος	*thliménos*
safe	ασφαλής	*asfalís*
safe (deposit box)	το χρηματοκιβώτιο	*to chrimatokivótyo*
safety pin	η παραμάνα	*i paramána*
sail	αρμενίζω	*armenízo*
sailing boat	το ιστιοφόρο	*to istiofóro*
salad oil	το λάδι	*to ládhi*
salad	η σαλάτα	*i saláta*
salami	το σαλάμι	*to salámi*
sale	το ξεπούλημα	*to xepóolima*
salt	το αλάτι	*to aláti*
same	ο ίδιος	*o ídhyos*
sandy beach	η πλαζ	*i plaz*
sanitary pad	η πετσέτα υγείας	*i petséta iyías*
sardines	οι σαρδέλες	*i sardhéles*
satisfied	πολύ ευχαριστημένος/η	*polí efcharistiménos/i*
Saturday	το Σάββατο	*to sávato*
sauce	η σάλτσα	*i sáltsa*
sauna	η σάουνα	*i sáoona*
sausage	το λουκάνικο	*to lookániko*
savoury	πικάντικος	*pikándikos*
say	λέγω	*légho*
scarf	το κασκόλ	*to kaskól*
scenic walk	η βόλτα	*i vólta*
school	το σχολείο	*to scholío*
scissors	το ψαλίδι	*to psalídhi*
scooter	η βεσπα	*i véspa*
scorpion	ο σκορπιός	*o skorpyós*
Scotland	η Σκωτία	*i skotía*
Scotsman/woman	ο Σκωτσέζος/η Σκωτσέζα	*o skotsézos/ i skotséza*
scrambled eggs	η στραπατσάδα	*i strapatsádha*
screw	η βίδα	*i vídha*
screwdriver	το κατσαβίδι	*to katsavídhi*
sculpture	η γλυπτική	*i ghliptikí*
sea	η θάλασσα	*i thálasa*
search	ψάχνω	*psáchno*
search for	ψάχνω	*psáchno*
seasickness	η ναυτία	*i naftía*
seat	η θέση	*i thési*
seatbelt	η ζώνη	*i zóni*
second	δεύτερος	*dhéfteros*
second (of time)	το δευτερόλεπτο	*to dhefterólepto*
second-hand	μεταχειρισμένος	*metahirizménos*
secretion	η έκκριση	*i ékrisi*
sedative	το ηρεμιστικό	*to iremistikó*
see	βλέπω	*vlépo*

self-timer (photo)	ο αυτορρυθμιζόμενος φωτοφράκτης	o aftorithmizómenos fotofráktis
semi-skimmed	ημίπαχο	imípacho
send	στέλνω	stélno
sentence	η πρόταση	i prótasi
September	ο Σεπτέμβριος	o septémvrios
serious	σοβαρός	sovarós
service	η εξυπηρέτηση	i exipirétisi
shade	ο ίσκιος	o ískyos
shallow	ρηχός	richós
shampoo	το σαμπουάν	to sampwán
shark	ο καρχαρίας	o karcharías
shave (verb)	ξυρίζω	xirízo
shaver	η ξυριστική μηχανή	i xiristikí michaní
shaving soap	το σαπούνι ξυρίσματος	to sapóoni xirízmatos
shaving brush	το πινέλο ξυρίσματος	to pinélo xirízmatos
shaving cream	η κρέμα ξυρίσματος	i kréma xirízmatos
sheet	το σεντόνι	to sendóni
sherry	το σέρυ	to séri
shirt	το πουκάμισο	to pookámiso
shoe	το παπούτσι	to papóotsi
shoe shop	το υποδηματοπωλείο, το παπουτσάδικο	to ipodhimatopolío, to papootstádhiko
shoe polish	το βερνίκι παπουτσιών	to verníki papootsyón
shoelace	το κορδόνι	to kordhóni
shop assistant	η πωλήτρια	i polítria
shop	το μαγαζί	to maghazí
shop window	η βιτρίνα	i vitrína
shop	ψωνίζω	psonízo
shopping centre	το εμπορικό κέντρο	to emborikó kéndro
short circuit	το βραχυκύκλωμα	to vrachikíkloma
short	κοντός	kondós
shortly	σε λίγο	se lígho
shoulder	ο ώμος	o ómos
show	η παράσταση	i parástasi
shower	το ντους	to doos
shutter	το παντζούρι	to padzóori
sick	άρρωστος	árostos
side of the street	η μεριά του δρόμου	i meryá too dhrómoo
sieve	το σουρωτήρι	to soorotíri
sign (verb)	υπογράφω	ipoghráfo
sign	η πινακίδα	i pinakídha
signature	η υπογραφή	i ipoghrafí
silence	η ησυχία	i isihía
silver	το ασήμι	to asími
silver-plated	επάργυρος	epáryiros
simple	απλός	aplós
single (ticket)	απλό εισιτήριο	apló isitírio
single (unmarried)	ανύπανδρος	anípandhros
single	μονός	monós
sister	η αδερφή	i adherfí
sit	κάθομαι	káthome
size	το νούμερο	to nóomero
skating	το πατινάζ	to patináz
skin rash	το εξάνθημα	to exánthima
skin	το δέρμα	to dhérma
skirt	η φούστα	i fóosta

sleep	κοιμάμαι	kimáme
sleeping pills	τα υπνωτικά	ta ipnotiká
sleeping car	το βαγκον-λί	to vagonlí
slides	τα σλάιτς	ta sláidz
slip (woman's)	το μεσοφόρι	to mesofóri
slow train	το αργό τρένο	to arghó tréno
small	μικρός	mikrós
small change	τα ψηλά	ta psilá
smell of (verb)	βρομώ	vromó
smoke	ο καπνός	o kapnós
smoke (verb)	καπνίζω	kapnízo
smoked	καπνιστός	kapnistós
smoking compartment	το βαγόνι καπνίσματος	to vaghóni kapnízmatos
snake	το φίδι	to fídhi
snorkel	ο αναπνευστήρας	o anapnevstíras
snow	το χιόνι	to hyóni
snowing, it is	χιονίζει	hyonízi
soap powder	η σαπουνόσκονη	i sapoonóskoni
soap	το σαπούνι	to sapóoni
soap dish	η σαπουνιέρα	i sapoonyéra
socket	η πρίζα	i príza
socks	οι κάλτσες	i káltses
soft drink	το αναψυκτικό	to anapsiktikó
soft toy	το ζωάκι (παιδιού)	to zoáki (pedhyóo)
sole	η σόλα	i sóla
sole (fish)	η γλώσσα	i ghlósa
someone	κάποιος	kápyos
sometimes	μερικές φορές	merikés forés
somewhere	κάπου	kápoo
son	ο γιος	o yos
soon	γρήγορα	ghríghora
sore throat	ο πονόλαιμος	o ponólemos
sorry	λυπάμαι	lipáme
sort/type	το είδος	to ídhos
soup	η σούπα	i sóopa
sour	ξινός	xinós
source	η πηγή	i piyí
south wind	ο νοτιάς	o notyás
souvenir	το σουβενίρ	to soovenír
spaghetti	τα μακαρόνια	ta makarónya
spanner	το γαλλικό κλειδί	to ghalikó klidhí
spare tyre	η ρεζέρβα	i rezérva
spare wheel	η ρόδα ρεζέρβα	i ródha rezérva
spare	η ρεζέρβα	i rezérva
spare	το ανταλλακτικό	to andalaktikó
spare parts	τα εξαρτήματα ρεζέρβας	ta exartímata rezérvas
speak	μιλάω	miláo
special	εξαιρετικός	exeretikós
specialist	ο ειδικός	o idhikós
speciality	η σπεσιαλιτέ	i spesialité
speed limit	η ανώτατη ταχύτητα	i anótati tahítita
spell	συλλαβίζω	silavízo
spicy	πικάντικος	pikándikos
splinter	η αγκίδα	angídha
spoon	το κουτάλι	to kootáli
sport	ο αθλητισμός	o athlitizmós

sports centre	το αθλητικό κέντρο	to athlitikó kéndro
sportsground	το γήπεδο	to yípedho
sprain	στραμπουλίζω	stramboolízo
spring	η άνοιξη	i ánixi
square	η πλατεία	i platía
square (shape)	το τετράγωνο	to tetrághono
square metre	το τετραγωνικό μέτρο	to tetraghonikó métro
squeeze (verb)	ζουλώ	zooló
stain	ο λεκές	o lekés
stairs	η σκάλα	i skála
stalls (theatre)	η πλατεία	i platía
stamp	το γραμματόσημο	to ghramatósimo
start	παίρνω μπρος	pérno bros
station	ο σταθμός	o stathmós
statue	το άγαλμα	to ághalma
stay	η διαμονή	i dhiamoní
stay (verb)	μένω	méno
steal	κλέβω	klévo
steel	το ατσάλι	to atsáli
stench	η μπόχα	i bócha
sticking plaster	ο λευκοπλάστης	o lefkoplástis
sting (verb)	τσιμπάω	tsimbáo
stitch (verb)	ράβω	rávo
stitches (medical)	τα ράμματα	ta rámata
stockings	οι κάλτσες	i káltses
stomachache	ο στομαχόπονος	o stomachóponos
stomach cramp	η κράμπα στην κοιλιά	i krámpa stingiliá
stomach	το στομάχι	to stomáchi
stools (medical)	τα κόπρανα	ta kóprana
stop	σταματάω	stamatáo
stop	η στάση	i stási
stopover	η ενδιάμεση προσγείωση	i endhiámesi prosyíosi
storm, there is a	έχει τρικυμία	ehí trikimía
storm	η θύελλα	i thíela
straight hair	ίσια μαλλιά	ísya malyá
straight ahead	ίσια	ísya
straw	το καλαμάκι	to kalamáki
strawberries	οι φράουλες	i fráooles
street	ο δρόμος, η οδός	o dhrómos, i odhós
strike	η απεργία	i aperyía
stroll around town	η βόλτα στην πόλη	i vólta stimbóli
strong	δυνατός	dhinatós
study	σπουδάζω	spoodházo
stuffing	η γέμιση	i yémisi
subtitled	με υπότιτλους	me ipotítloos
succeed	τα καταφέρνω	ta kataférno
sugar	η ζάχαρη	i záchari
sugar cubes	οι κύβοι ζάχαρης	i kívi zácharis
suit	το κοστούμι	to kostóomi
suitcase	η βαλίτσα	i valítsa
summer time	η καλοκαιρινή ώρα	i kalokyeriní óra
summer	το καλοκαίρι	to kalokyéri
sun hat	το καπέλο ηλίου	to kapélo ilíoo
sun	ο ήλιος	o ílyos
sunbathing	η ηλιοθεραπεία	i ilyotherapía
Sunday	η Κυριακή	i kiryakí

15

sunglasses	τα μαύρα γυαλιά	ta mávra yalyá
sunrise	η ανατολή	i anatolí
sunset	το ηλιοβασίλεμα	to ilyovasílema
sunstroke	η ηλίαση	i ilíasi
suntan lotion	η κρέμα ηλίου	i kréma ilíoo
suntan oil	το λάδι ηλίου	to ládhi ilíoo
supermarket	η υπεραγορά	i iperaghorá
surcharge	το συμπληρωματικό ποσόν	to simpliromatikó posón
surf board	η σανίδα του σερφ	i sanídha too serf
surfing	το σέρφιγκ	to sérfing
surname	το επώνυμο	to epónimo
surprise	η έκπληξη	i ékplixi
swallow (verb)	καταπίνω	katapíno
swamp	το τέλμα	to télma
sweat	ο ιδρώτας	o idhrótas
sweet	γλυκός	ghlikós
sweetcorn	το καλαμπόκι	to kalambóki
sweets	οι καραμέλες	i karaméles
swim (verb)	κολυμπώ	kolimbó
swimming pool	η πισίνα	i pisína
swimming costume	το μαγιό	to mayó
swindle	η απάτη	i apáti
switch	ο διακόπτης	o dhiakóptis
synagogue	η συναγωγή	i sinaghoyí

T

table	το τραπέζι	to trapézi
table tennis	το πινγκ πονγκ	to ping pong
tablet	το χάπι	to chápi
take (photograph)	βγάζω	vgházo
take	παίρνω	pérno
take (verb, of time)	διαρκώ/κρατώ	dhiarkó/krató
take pictures	φωτογραφίζω	fotoghrafízo
talcum powder	το ταλκ	to talk
talk	μιλάω	miláo
tampon	το ταμπόν	to tampón
tap water	το νερό της βρύσης	to neró tis vrísis
tap	η βρύση	i vrísi
taste	δοκιμάζω	dhokimázo
tasty	νόστιμος	nóstimos
tax-free shop	το μαγαζί αφορολόγητων ειδών	to maghazí aforolóyiton idhón
taxi	το ταξί	to taxí
taxi stand	η στάση ταξί	i stási taxí
teaspoon	το κουταλάκι	to kootaláki
tea	το τσάι	to tsái
teapot	η τσαγιέρα	i tsayéra
tee shirt	η φανέλα	i fanéla
telegram	το τηλεγράφημα	to tileghráfima
telephone receiver	το ακουστικό	to akoostikó
telephone number	ο αριθμός τηλεφώνου	o arithmós tilefónoo
telescopic lens	ο τηλεφακός	o tilefakós
television	η τηλεόραση	i tileórasi
telex	το τηλέτυπο	to tilétipo
temperature	η θερμοκρασία	i thermokrasía

temporary filling	το προσωρινό σφράγγισμα	*to prosorinó sfráyizma*
temporary	προσωρινός	*prosorinós*
tender	μαλακός	*malakós*
tennis ball	η μπάλα του τένις	*i bála too ténis*
tennis	το τένις	*to ténis*
tennis racket	η ρακέτα του τένις	*i rakéta too ténis*
tennis court	το γήπεδο τένις	*to yípedho ténis*
tent	η σκηνή	*i skiní*
tent peg	το πασαλάκι της σκηνής	*to pasaláki tis skinís*
terrible	φοβερός	*foverós*
thank you	ευχαριστώ	*efcharistó*
thank (verb)	ευχαριστώ	*efcharistó*
thaw	λιώνω	*lióno*
the same	το ίδιο	*to ídhyo*
theatre	το θέατρο	*to théatro*
theft	η κλοπή	*i klopí*
there	εκεί	*ekí*
thermometer	το θερμόμετρο	*to thermómetro*
thick	χοντρός	*chondrós*
thief	ο κλέφτης	*o kléftis*
thigh	το μπούτι	*to bóoti*
thin	λεπτός, αδύνατος	*leptós, adhínatos*
things	τα πράματα	*ta prámata*
think (verb)	νομίζω	*nomízo*
third	το τρίτο	*to tríto*
thirst	η δίψα	*i dhípsa*
this morning	σήμερα το πρωί	*símera to proí*
this evening	απόψε	*apópse*
this afternoon	σήμερα το απόγευμα	*símera to apóyevma*
thread	η κλωστούλα, η κλωστή	*i klostóola, i klostí*
throat lozenges	οι παστίλιες για το λαιμό	*i pastílyes ya to lemó*
throat	ο λαιμός	*o lemós*
throw up (be sick)	κάνω εμετό	*káno emetó*
thunderstorm	η καταιγίδα	*i kateyídha*
Thursday	η Πέμπτη	*i pémpti*
ticket	το εισιτήριο	*to isitírio*
tidy up (verb)	μαζεύω	*mazévo*
tie	η γραβάτα	*i ghraváta*
tights	το καλτσόν	*to kaltsón*
time	η ώρα	*i óra*
times	φορές	*forés*
timetable	το δρομολόγιο	*to dhromolóyo*
tinned food	η κονσέρβα	*i konsérva*
tip	το πουρμπουάρ	*to poorbwáar*
tissues	τα χαρτομάντηλα	*ta chartomándila*
to let	νοικιάζεται	*nikyázete*
toast (French-style)	η φρυγανιά	*i frighanyá*
tobacco	ο καπνός	*o kapnós*
tobacco (loose)	ο καπνός	*o kapnós*
tobacconist's	το καπνοπωλείο	*to kapnopolío*
today	σήμερα	*símera*
toe	το δάχτυλο	*to dháchtilo*
together	μαζί	*mazí*

toilet	η τουαλέτα	i twaléta
toilet paper	το χαρτί υγείας	to chartí iyías
toiletries	τα είδη τουαλέτας	ta ídhi twalétas
tomato puree	ο ντοματοπολτός	o domatopoltós
tomato	η ντομάτα	i domáta
tomato sauce	το κέτσαπ	to kétsap
tomorrow	αύριο	ávrio
tongue	η γλώσσα	i ghlósa
tonic water	το τόνικ	to tónik
tonight	απόψε	apópse
too	επίσης	epísis
tooth	το δόντι	to dhóndi
toothache	ο πονόδοντος	o ponódhondos
toothbrush	η οδοντόβουρτσα	i odhondóvoortsa
toothpaste	η οδοντόπαστα	i odhondópasta
toothpick	η οδοντογλυφίδα	i odhondoghlifídha
torch	ο φακός	o fakós
total	το σύνολο	to sínolo
tough	σκληρός	sklirós
tour guide	ο ξεναγός	o xenaghós
tour boat	το εκδρομικό καραβάκι	to ekdhromikó karaváki
tourist card	η τουριστική κάρτα	tooristikí kárta
tourist class	η τουριστική θέση	i tooristikí thési
tourist menu	το τουριστικό μενού	to tooristikó menóo
Tourist Information Office	το τουριστικό γραφείο	to tooristikó ghrafío
tow rope	το σκοινί τραβήγματος	to skiní travíghmatos
tow	τραβάω	traváo
towel	η πετσέτα	i petséta
tower	ο πύργος	o pírghos
town-hall	το δημαρχείο	to dhimarchio
toys	τα παιχνίδια	ta pechnídhya
traffic light	το φανάρι	to fanári
traffic	η κυκλοφορία	i kikloforía
train ticket	το εισιτήριο τρένου	to isitírio trénoo
train	το τρένο	to tréno
trainers	τα παπούτσια αθλητισμού	ta papóotsya athlitizmóo
translate	μεταφράζω	metafrázo
travel agent	το πρακτορείο ταξιδίων	to praktorío taxidhíon
travel	ταξιδεύω	taxidhévo
traveller	ο ταξιδιώτης	taxidhyótis
traveller's cheque	η ταξιδιωτική επιταγή	i taxidhyotikí epitayí
treacle	το σιρόπι	to sirópi
treatment	η θεραπεία	i therapía
triangle	το τρίγωνο	to tríghono
trim (verb)	ψαλιδίζω	psalidhízo
trip	το ταξίδι	to taxídhi
trousers	το παντελόνι	to pandelóni
trout	η πέστροφα	i péstrofa
trunk (call)	υπεραστικός	iperastikós
try on	δοκιμάζω	dhokimázo
tube	το σωληνάριο	to solinário
Tuesday	η Τρίτη	i tríti
tumble drier	το στεγνωτήριο	to steghnotírio
tuna	ο τόννος	o tónos

Word list

15

tunnel	το τούνελ	to tóonel
TV guide	ο οδηγός ραδιοφώνου/ τηλεόρασης	o odhighós radhiofónoo/tileórasis
tweezers	το τσιμπιδάκι	to tsimbidháki
tyre	το εξωτερικό λάστιχο	to exoterikó lásticho
tyre pressure	η πίεση λάστιχων	i píesi lástichon
tyre lever	ο μοχλός για την αφαίρεση λάστιχων	o mochlós ya tin aféresi lástichon

U

ugly	άσχημος	áschimos
ulcer	το έλκος	to élkos
umbrella	η ομπρέλα	i ombréla
under	κάτω από	káto apó
underground	το μετρό	to metró
underground train system	το δίκτυο του μετρό	to díktio too metró
underground station	ο σταθμός του μετρό	o stathmós too metró
underpants (ladies')	το σλιπάκι	to slipáki
underpants	το σώβρακο	to sóvrako
understand	καταλαβαίνω	katalavéno
underwear	τα εσώρουχα	ta esóroocha
undress	γδύνω	ghdhíno
unemployed	άνεργος	ánerghos
uneven	άνισος	ánisos
university	το πανεπιστήμιο	to panepistímio
unleaded	αμόλυβδος	amólivdhos
urgency	η βιασύνη	i viasíni
urgent	επείγον	epíghon
urine	τα ούρα	to óora
use (verb)	χρησιμοποιώ	chrisimopyó
usually	συνήθως	siníthos
utensil (cooking)	το σκεύος	to skévos

V

vacate	αδειάζω	adhyázo
vaccinate	εμβολιάζω	emvolyázo
vagina	ο κόλπος	o kólpos
vaginal infection	η κολπική μόλυνση	i kolpikí mólinsi
valid	έγκυρος	éngkiros
valley	η κοιλάδα, το λαγκάδι	i kiládha, to langádhi
valuable	πολύτιμος	polítimos
van	το φορτηγάκι	to fortigháki
vanilla	η βανίλια	i vanílya
vase	το βάζο	to vázo
vaseline	η βαζελίνη	i vazelíni
veal	το μοσχαρίσιο κρέας	to moscharísyo kréas
vegetable soup	η χορτόσουπα	i chortósoopa
vegetables	τα λαχανικά	ta lachaniká
vegetarian	ο χορτοφάγος	o chortofághos
vein	η φλέβα	i fléva
venereal disease	το αφροδίσιο νόσημα	to afrodhísyo nósima
vest	η φανέλλα	i fanéla
via	μέσω	méso
video recorder	το βίντεο	to vídeo
videotape	η βιντεοταινία	i videotenía
view	η θέα	i théa

village festival/fair	το πανηγύρι	to paniyíri
village woman	η χωριάτισσα	i choriátisa
village	το χωριό	to choryó
viral infection	η ίωση	i íosi
visa	η βίζα	i víza
visit	η επίσκεψη	i epískepsi
visit (verb)	επισκέπτομαι	episképtome
visiting time	η ώρα επίσκεψης	i óra episképsis
vitamin pills	τα χάπια βιταμίνης	ta chápya vitamínis
vitamin	η βιταμίνη	i vitamíni
volcano	το ηφαίστειο	to iféstio
volleyball	το βόλλεϋ	to vólei
vomit	κάνω εμετό	káno emetó

W

wait for	περιμένω	periméno
waiter	το γκαρσόνι	to garsóni
waiting room	η αίθουσα αναμονής	i éthoosa anamonís
waitress	η σερβιτόρα	i servitóra
wake up	ξυπνάω	xipnáo
Wales	η Ουαλλία	i walía
walk	ο περίπατος	o perípatos
walk (verb)	περπατώ	perpató
wallet	το πορτοφόλι	to portofóli
wardrobe	η γκαρντ-ρόμπα	i gard-róba
warm	θερμός, ζεστός	thermós, zestós
warn	προειδοποιώ	proidhopió
warning	η προειδοποίηση	i proidhopíisi
wash	πλένω	pléno
washing machine	το πλυντήριο	to plindírio
washing	η μπουγάδα	i booghádha
washing powder	το απορρυπαντικό	to aporipandikó
washing line	το σκοινί μπουγάδας	to skiní booghádhas
wasp	η σφήκα	i sfíka
water	το νερό	to neró
water-ski	το θαλάσσιο σκι	to thalásio ski
waterfall	ο καταρράχτης	o katarráchtis
waterproof	αδιάβροχος	adhiávrochos
wave-pool	πισίνα με κύματα	pisína me kímata
waves	τα κύματα	ta kímata
way (road)	ο δρόμος	o dhrómos
way	η κατεύθυνση	i katéthinsi
way, on the	στο δρόμο	sto dhrómo
we	εμείς	emís
weak	αδύνατος	adhínatos
weather	ο καιρός	o kyerós
weather forecast	το μετεωρολογικό δελτίο	to meteoroloyikó dheltío
wedding	ο γάμος	o ghámos
Wednesday	η Τετάρτη	i tétarti
week	η εβδομάδα	i evdhomádha
weekend	το σαββατοκύριακο	to savatokíryakoadh
weekly ticket	η εβδομαδιαία κάρτα	evdhomiéa kárta
welcome	καλώς ήρθατε	kalós írthate
well done (cooking)	καλοψημένος	kalopsiménos
well	καλά	kalá
well	καλός	kalós

143

west (to the)	δυτικά	dhitiká
wet	υγρός	ighrós
wet-suit	το κοστούμι του σερφ	to kostóomi too serf
what?	τί;	ti?
wheel	η ρόδα	i ródha
wheelchair	το καροτσάκι (αναπήρων)	to karotsáki (anapíron)
when?	πότε;	póte?
where?	πού;	poo?
which?	ποιός;	pyos?
whipped cream	η σαντιγί	i santiyí
white	άσπρος	áspros
who?	ποιός;	pyos?
why?	γιατί;	yatí?
wide-angle lens	ο ευρυγώνιος φακός	o evrighónyos fakós
widow	η χήρα	i híra
widower	ο χήρος	o híros
wife	η γυναίκα	i yinéka
wind	ο άνεμος	o ánemos
windbreak	ο ανεμοφράκτης	o anemofráchtis
window	το παράθυρο	to paráthiro
window (booking office, bank)	η θυρίδα	i thirídha
wine	το κρασί	to krasí
wine list	ο κατάλογος κρασιών	o katáloghos krasyón
winter	ο χειμώνας	o himónas
witness	ο μάρτυρας	o mártiras
woman	η γυναίκα	i yinéka
wonderful	θαυμάσιος	thavmásios
wood	το ξύλο	to xílo
wool	το μαλλί	to malí
word	η λέξη	i léxi
work	η δουλειά	dhoolyiá
working day	η εργάσιμη ημέρα	i erghásimi méra
workout	η άσκηση	i áskisi
worn	τριμμένος	triménos
worried	ανήσυχος	anísichos
wound	η πληγή	i pliyí
wrap	τυλίγω	tilígho
wrist	ο καρπός	o karpós
write	γράφω	ghráfo
write down	καταγράφω	kataghráfo
writing paper	το χαρτί αλληλογραφίας	to chartí aliloghrafías
written document	γραπτά	ghraptá
wrong	λάθος	láthos

Y

yacht	το γιωτ	to yot
year	ο χρόνος	o chrónos
yellow	κίτρινος	kítrinos
yes	ναι	ne
yesterday	χτες	chtes
yoghurt	το γιαούρτι	to yaóorti
you	εσείς	esís
youth hostel	ο ξενώνας νεότητας	o xenónas neótitas

z

zip	το φερμουάρ	*to fermwár*
zoo	ο ζωολογικός κήπος	*o zo-oloyikós kípos*

Basic grammar

1 The Greek alphabet

(See also 1.8 Telephone alphabet)

a	A	álfa	somewhere between **a** in **mast** and **u** in **cup**
ß	B	víta	as **v** in **van**
γ	Γ	gháma	as **y** in **yet** before **e** and **i** sounds; before any other sound, a hard **g** (as in **grab**) as far down your throat as possible. (This sound is shown as **gh** in the transcriptions.)
δ	Δ	dhélta	as hard **th** in **this**
ε	E	épsilon	as **e** in **met**
ζ	Z	zíta	as **z** in **zoo**
η	H	íta	as **i** in **quarantine** (i.e. like the **ee** in **feet**)
θ	Θ	thíta	as soft **th** in **thin**
ι	I	yóta	as **i** in **quarantine** (i.e. like **ee** in **feet**), but before another vowel often becomes **y**- as in **yacht**)
κ	K	kápa	as **k** in **kitchen**, but before **e**- and **i**-sounds, more like **ky**)
λ	Λ	lámdha	as **l** in **lick**
μ	M	mi	as **m** in **mat**
ν	N	ni	as **n** in **not**
ξ	Ξ	xi	as **x** in **box**
o	O	ómikron	as **o** in **pop**
π	Π	pi	as **p** in **pin**
ρ	P	ro	closer to a Scots **r** than an English one
σ,ς	Σ	síghma	like a soft English **s** as in **sit**, except before the sounds **b,gh,dh** and **m**, when it is like **z**
τ	T	taf	as **t** in **tin**
υ	Y	ípsilon	as **i** in **quarantine** (i.e. like the **ee** in **feet**)
φ	Φ	fi	as **f** in **fit**
χ	X	hi	as **h** in **hat** before **i** or **e** sounds; before any other sound, as Scots **ch** in **loch**
ψ	Ψ	psi	as combination of **p** and **s** in **tops**
ω	Ω	omégha	as **o** in **pop**

2 Vowels

There are only five vowels sounds in Greek, approximating to the English sounds a (see α), e (see ε), ee (see ι), o (see o) and oo as in foot (spelt ou), but several of these sounds can be written in a number of ways:

ε, αι both = **e** in **met**
η, ι, υ, ει, οι = **i** in **quarantine** (ie. like **ee** in **feet**)
o, ω = o in pot
N.B. αυ and ευ are pronounced **av** and **ev** before ß, γ, δ, ζ, λ, μ, ν, ρ, τ or another vowel; before anything else they are pronounced **f**. Thus **αυγό** (egg) is pronounced *avghó* but **απόλαυση** (enjoyment) is pronounced *apólafsi*.

3 The consonant combinations

As well as the single consonant sounds indicated above in the description of the alphabet, there are a number of sounds which can only be written with two consonants together. These are:

b as in **bet** = μπ
d as in **dog** = ντ
g as in **gap** = γκ.

Similarly, when one word ends in the sound n and the next begins with the sound p, t, or k the following changes occur:
τον πατέρα (ton patéra - the father) becomes *tombatéra*
την ταβέρνα (tin tavérna - the taverna) becomes *tindavrna*
τον καταλογο (ton katálogho) becomes *tongatálogho*.

The following combinations of consonants also make particular sounds:
γγ = **ng** as in **sing**
γξ = **n(g)x** – somewhere between **things** and **thinks**
γχ = **n(g)ch** – try pronouncing the middle of **melancholy** with a Scots **ch** after the **n**. Fortunately, the last two combinations are relatively rare!

4 Stress and accents

The accents on Greek words indicate where the stress goes. In the pronunciation guide the stresses are also marked with an accent, e.g. **o πατέρας** = *o patéras*. The vowel **ou** is transcribed as **oo** when not stressed and **óo** when stressed.
N.B. Any two other vowels together in the transcription must be pronounced separately, e.g. **αεροδρόμιο** must be pronounced *a-e-rodhrómyo*.

5 Nouns

Greek nouns each have a gender, which can be masculine, feminine or neuter. They also have endings which change to show whether they are singular or plural, and whether they are nominative, accusative or genetive case. The nominative case is always used for the subject of an action; the accusative is used for the direct object of an action and after most prepositions (in, to, for etc.); the genetive is used to show possession (of someone or something) or indirect objects (to someone or something).

The most common forms are as follows:
masculine nouns have a singular nominative ending in: **-ος,-ας** or **-ης**
a corresponding plural nominative endings in: **-οι -ες -ες**
feminine nouns have a singular nominative ending in: **-η** or **-α**
a plural nominative ending in: **-ες**
neuter nouns have a singular nominative ending in: **-ο, -ι,** or **-α**
a corresponding plural nominative ending in: **-α, -ια -ατα**

In a brief introduction to Greek grammar it is not possible to give all the details of all the categories of nouns. Here are three common nouns in all the cases of both singular and plural, with the definite article (the):

	masculine singular	masculine plural
nominative (subject case)	ο δρόμος (the road)	οι δρόμοι
accusative (direct object case)	τον δρόμο	τους δρόμους
genetive (indirect object case)	του δρόμου	των δρόμων
	feminine singular	feminine plural
nominative (subject case)	η γυναίκα (woman)	οι γυναίκες
accusative (direct object case)	τη(ν) γυναίκα	τις γυναίκες
genetive (indirect object case)	της γυναίκας	των γυναίκων
	neuter singular	neuter plural
nominative (subject case)	το παιδί (child)	τα παιδιά
accusative (direct object case)	το παιδί	τα παιδιά
genetive (indirect object case)	του παιδιού	ού των παιδιών

N.B. Like nouns the definite article (the) also has, as can be seen from the above examples, three genders and nine cases. It must always agree with its noun in number, gender and case.Christian names, names of countries, days of the week and months all take a definite article in front of them, eg. **ο Γιάννης** (John), **η Αγγλία** (England), **η Παρασκευή** (Friday), **ο Μάιος** (May).

6 Adjectives

Adjectives in Greek behave like the definite article: they agree in gender, number and case with the noun which they describe. The most common form of adjective has endings which are similar to those of the nouns:

	masc. singular	fem. singular	neut. singular
nominative (subject case)	-ος	-α/-η	-ο
accusative (direct object case)	-ο	-α/-η	-ο
genetive (indirect object case)	-ου	-ας/-ης	-ου
	masc. plural	fem. plural	neut. plural
nominative (subject case)	-οι	-ες	-α
accusative (direct object case)	-ους	-ες	-α
genetive (indirect object case)	-ων	-ων	-ων

Adjectives usually stand before their noun, as in English.
The words **αυτός** (this) and **εκείνος** (that) also function as adjectives,
but they stand before the definite article. So this beautiful house and of
that beautiful woman in Greek are: **αυτό το ωραίο σπίτι** and **εκείνος της
ωραίας γυναίκας.**

7 Verbs

Verbs in Greece are very complex. They are made up of two parts: the
stem, which gives the main idea of the verb (eg. have, want, drink), and
the ending, which shows whether the action is singular or plural, first,
second or third person, and past or present. So in the verb **πληρώνω**
(pay), the stem is **πληρών-** (the idea of payment) and the ending **-ω**
shows that the action is first person singular and present tense. There
are two stems for most verbs, and also different sets of endings for
active and passive. It is obviously not possible to give more than very
basic information in a brief introduction like this. Below is the present
tense (active) of the verbs **έχω** (have) and **Θέλω** (want), divided up to
show the standard endings.

I have	**έχ-ω**	(écho)	I want	**Θέλ-ω**	(thélo)
You have	**έχ-εις**	(éhis)	You want	**Θέλ-εις**	(thélis)
He/she/it has	**έχ-ει**	(éhi)	He/she/it wants	**Θέλ-ει**	(théli)
We have	**έχ-ουμε**	(échoome)	We want	**Θέλ-ουμε**	(théloome)
You have	**έχ-ετε**	(éhete)	You want	**Θέλ-ετε**	(thélete)
They have	**έχ-ουν**	(échoon)	They want	**Θέλ-ουν**	(théloon)

8 Personal pronouns

As we have seen no separate word for I, you, we etc. is necessary to
show the subject of an action, as the ending of the verb gives you this
information. The object forms of the personal pronoun are as follows:
me = **με**, you (sing.) = **σε**, him = **τον**, her = **τη**, it = **τον, τη** or **το**
(according to the gender) we = **μας**, you (plur.) = **σας**, they = **τους** (for
people) or **τους** or **τα** (for things). These forms stand before the verb,
eg. **το Θέλω** (I want it). To say my, your, his etc., use the following
forms after the noun: my = **μου**, your (sing.) = **σου**, his = **του**, her = **της**,
our = **μας**, your (plur.) = **σας**, their = **τους** (for people and things): eg. **τα
παιδιά μας** = our children.

9 Prepositions

The most common prepositions are **για** (for), **από** (from) and **σε** (in or
to). They are all followed by the accusative case, eg. **από την Αθήνα**
(from Athens), **για τον φίλο μου** (for my friend). The preposition **σε**
contracts with the definite article in the following ways: **σε+τον = στον,
σε+την = στην, σε+το = στο,** eg. **στο Λονδίνο** (in London).